Forgiveness
Healing
Dreams
and Visions

By
Dorothy Coleman

Thank You.

Love
Dorothy Coleman

1

Printed in the USA
by Homeland Publishing

This book is dedicated to the Father, Son, and the Holy Ghost. To my wonderful husband, Albert Coleman, who stood by me faithfully through my labor and delivery of this project. I would like also to dedicate this book to my mother, Florence Hubbard, who passed away in 1996.

I would like to thank Denton and Elizebeth for their advice and encouragement.

Thanks also to Grandma Vern, Trudy, J.J., John, Darlene Campbell and Eve Sandy.

Since the Bible indicates that in the last days God will visit us through dreams and visions, *And it shall come to pass in the last days, saith God, I will pour out of my spirit upon all flesh: and your sons and your daughters shall prophesy, and your young men shall see visions, and your old men shall dream dreams.* (Acts 2:17)

3

Table of Contents

Introduction

In 1952 my mom, brother, and myself moved to California after my dad passed away. I was ten years old at the time, and my brother James was eight years old. My mother took a job to support us. I took a job baby sitting sometimes, and my brother had a job selling papers. We stayed busy, and we never got into any trouble because we had a praying mother. My mother would come home from work many times so tired, but she never forgot to teach us the word of God. We always had plenty of food to eat. We always had nice clothes to wear. My brother would go to the playground and play ball with his friends. After school I would come home and do my homework, and cook later. I never liked to hang out with many people. When I got off the school bus, I went home.

I went all the way through school. I finished high school in 1961, and attended college for two years. In 1963 I married my first husband, and later two sons were born. My first child, Mike, was born in 1964. In 1966, my second son, Jerry, was born. After that I went to work for about two years as a typist. Later down the road we divorced, but the Lord was with me. I raised my two sons to love the Lord. I asked my mother, Why did this happen to me? I was a good girl, I never gave you any trouble. My mother said to me, Sometimes we do not understand why some things happen in life, but I do know that the Lord is in control. That's why I love the Lord so much, and my mom, because I could trust them.

In 1968 I met my second husband, Al, and in 1969 we were married. He is from Alabama, and the third of fifteen children. We never had children together. But he loved my children so much. He worked two eight hour jobs to send them to Christian school.

Al loves the Lord very much. We took the children to church every Sunday. They were in many church programs. Al took them to choir practice every Saturday morning. Al and I also sang in the adult choir. We would visit the sick and pray for them. All of us did this, Al, myself, my mom and the children. We were very active in the church.

We were in the Methodist Church. We loved the preaching, singing and much more. But still there was something missing in my life. I came home from work one day when I was a teacher's aid working with the first grade. I raised my arms toward Heaven and cried out to God, I need more of You, and I was crying. I had one of those televisions with UHF antenna, they call them rabbit ears. We had only about three or four channels, but I never did watch UHF, but something told me to turn there. I saw this blonde hair lady talking about Jesus, and she was crying, so I put every thing down to listen to her talk about how much Jesus loved me. Then I started crying too. After that, I could not wait to come home from work. I would turn to the UHF channel; I was thirsty for more. So the next day I came home wanting to know more about Jesus. I saw this man named Dwight Thompson talking about Hell, and that really caught my attention. I know now that it was the Holy Spirit telling me to turn to the UHF channel, and that the lady I saw that first day was Jan Crouch.

In 1975 I asked Jesus to come into my heart, and I became a Born-Again Christian.

John 3:3—Jesus said *verily, verily, I say unto thee, except a man be born again, he cannot see the Kingdom of God.* So I asked Jesus to forgive me of all my sins, and to come into my heart. I told Al and the children. We had been going to church every Sunday, but we had never asked Jesus to come into our lives. So I asked them all, and they said yes, so we all knelt and prayed.

My Life Changed

My whole life changed after I became a Born-Again Christian. One night I was praying and praising the Lord; I was so happy I cried myself to sleep. The next thing I knew, I saw this very tall person walk into my room. He came and stood beside my bed, and he was looking at me. I never saw such a beautiful smile. He then put his hand on my head and I felt like electricity go all over my body, and I could not move. He had on a long white robe, I could not see his face real well, his hair came down to his neck. I knew that it was Jesus. He came to give me <u>peace</u>, and to <u>baptize</u> me with the <u>Holy Ghost</u>.

John 14:26—*But the Comforter, which is the Holy Ghost, whom the Father will send in my name, he shall teach you all things, and bring all things to your remembrance, whatsoever I have said unto you.*

V 27 *Peace I leave with you, my peace I give unto you: not as the world giveth, give I unto you. Let not your heart be troubled, neither let it be afraid.*

On Sunday when we went to church, Al and I went

downstairs to eat breakfast. After the first service we were all sitting at the table with the people who sing in the choir with us, and Pastor Ed. I explained to Pastor Ed about the vision of Jesus coming into my room, and he asked me if I spoke in tongues, and I said no. So he told me to close my eyes. He put his hand on my shoulder, and he told me not to pay attention to everyone around me, but to keep my mind on Jesus. So I did, and when I did my spirit left my body and went straight to the <u>Throne</u>. When I came back, I was speaking in other languages. All the people sitting at the table with me said, Dorothy, you were speaking in <u>tongues</u>.

I got up and I felt like I wanted to fall down. I was going from side to side. Al said, When we get home, I am going to bake you a cake. I said to him, I do not want any cake. I have something better than cake.

That night when I went to bed, I was speaking in another language, <u>Japanese</u>. God spoke to me, saying, It is well with my soul.

I was sharing this with my mom, and she said, Not everyone can say it is well with their soul. But she did not understand the vision of Jesus coming into my room. She said, Is my daughter getting ready to die? I said, No, mom, your daughter is getting ready to live. And after I explained the scriptures to her, she believed me.

For people who do not understand Jesus coming into my room—Jesus still appears to people today. After His resurrection He appeared first to Mary Magdalene. You can see this in Matthew 28:1.

Mark 16:12,13—*After that, he appeared in another form unto two of them, as they walked and went into the country. And they went and told it unto the residue, but they did not believe.*

Jesus said to me, when I share my testimony, I do not have to prove myself to anyone.

Mark 16:14—*Afterward, he appeared unto the eleven as they sat at meat, and upbraided them with their unbelief and hardness of heart, because they believed not them which had* seen him after he was risen.

And their eyes were opened, and they knew him; and he vanished out of their sight—on the road to Emmaus. (Luke 24:31) They did not recognize Jesus. (Jesus comes in all forms.)

John 21:1—*After these things Jesus showed himself again to his disciples at the Sea of Ti-be-rias.*

After I saw the vision of Jesus, my spirit went to the Throne.

Psalm 11:4—*The Lord is in his Holy Temple, the Lord's throne is in heaven: his eyes behold, his eyelids try the children of men.*

Then I received my prayer language speaking in tongues.

1 Corinthians 14:2—*For he that speaketh in an unknown tongue speaketh not unto men, but unto God: for no man understandeth him; howbeit in the spirit he speaketh mysteries.*

Acts 2:1, 3, 4—*When the day of Pentecost was fully come, they were all with one accord in one place.*

And there appeared unto them cloven tongues like as of fire, and it sat upon each of them.

And they were all filled with the Holy Ghost, and began to speak with other tongues, as the spirit gave them utterance.

Pastor Ed Smith laid hands on me,

Acts 8:17—*Then laid they their hands on them, and they received the Holy Ghost.*

I just wanted to do something for Jesus, because I love Him so much. I started a Bible Study in my home.

I would like to share this wonderful letter with you that my older son wrote to the parents:

The Bible is the most wonderful storybook ever written. It is full of stories, all the way from the first chapter of Genesis to the last chapter of Revelation.

11

Because in countless homes family worship and the reading of the Bible have been neglected, and parents themselves seldom open its pages, a whole generation is growing up with little or no knowledge of this wonderful book.

Most children have heard little or nothing about the great Bible characters of ancient times. Their heroes are not Daniel, Paul, and Peter, but cartoons and superman. They have never heard of the love of Jesus. They have been robbed of the greatest treasure their minds and hearts could possess. No wonder there is so much juvenile delinquency, youthful vandalism, and lawlessness.

Boys and girls all around the world would love their parents, teachers, friends and everyone if they will study the Bible. The Bible is full of love.

After my son wrote this letter, and we prayed and passed them out to the parents, and all the parents signed the letters. Praise the Lord!

We started out with twenty children coming to our home every week for Bible study. We had to add on another room.

I would always pray with the boys and girls, first in the living room, then we would move to the den to start Bible Study. One day when I started to pray, this little boy, John, was talking, and I said, John, you know that you are not to talk while I am praying. But he said, Mrs. Coleman, I just wanted to tell you, Jesus is standing next to you, and when you walked across the room, he was walking next to you. I could hardly speak. So I asked him, what is he doing now? He said, he is standing with his arms stretched out and his feet across the other one.

Believe me, I could hardly teach that evening. I started to cry.

I also asked the principal at the school where I was working, if I could pray with the boys and girls after school. He said check back with me in about three days, because he had to check with the district first, but I knew in my heart that they were going to say no; and they did. But that did not stop me.

There was a man coming to the school every year passing out Bibles, but he had to stand outside the gate to pass them out.

One day we had an assembly at the school, a rock group was there. I did not attend. You could hear loud music all over the school, so I went over to the work room to run off some copies for my reading group, May I Come In. We had ditto machines back then to duplicate or copy something. I put the paper in, went back to class, with the paper in front of me. I started to cry. I said, Lord, they want everything else in school except You. Then I put the paper in my desk. In the next ten minutes the children came in so hyper it was time for them to go home.

On Monday I was sitting in my reading group when I took the paper out of my desk, but I did not look at it. I was holding the paper in front of me, showing it to the children and getting ready to explain to them concerning their lesson. Then

13

one of the children said, Mrs. Coleman, there is a cross on your paper. I turned the paper around, and there was the cross. The children were making so much noise, the teacher on the other side came over and asked, What is going on over here? I showed him the paper. He looked at it and said, How did that get there? I tried to explain it to him, but he did not understand. What happened is that when I had put my head down and started crying that day, and said to the Lord, They want everything else in this school but not Jesus, and if you notice on the paper there is a cross. The reading book was about Country Mouse, and City Mouse, *May I Come In.*

So the Lord was showing me, He wants to come into the schools.

Jesus appeared on my paper at school.

Acts 2:16-19—*But this is that which was spoken by the prophet Joel:*

And it shall come to pass in the last days, saith God, I will pour out of my spirit upon all flesh: and your sons and your <u>daughters shall prophesy,</u> and your young men shall see <u>visions,</u> and your old men shall <u>dream dreams</u>:

And on my servants and on my handmaidens I will pour in those days I will pour out in those days my spirit: and they shall prophesy.

And I will show wonders in heaven above, and signs in the <u>earth beneath; blood, and fire, and vapor of smoke</u>.

The Cross That Appeared On My Paper

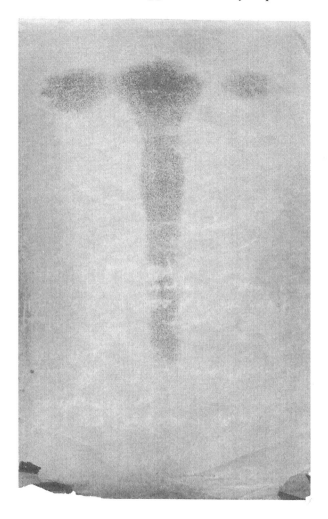

The City Mouse And The Country Mouse

may ← Come In

] the City

into the   ?

going |

y Mou:

ood do

The First Healing

I was on the radio when I lived in California, sharing about the cross. Even at church on Sunday, I was showing the cross on the paper and sharing about it. And when I finished, this little girl told me that when I was sharing about the cross, there were two big angels standing on each side of me. And she said, While you are sitting down, they are still standing near you.

I had a vision I was with my angel. She was a tall, thin beautiful black lady. We were inside a big beautiful building with lots of people and she said, Dorothy, let's go outside. So I followed her. When I stepped outside the grass did not look like the grass here; I can't explain it. Then I looked up, and saw this handsome young man, and I knew who he was. I said to him, you are Gabriel. He looked at me and smiled, shook his head yes, but he never said a word. Gabriel in the Bible is one of the archangels chosen as a special messenger of God.

So I went everywhere praying for people because God is so good, and I wanted to do more for Him.

I remember one Sunday after church, my mom, my husband, two children that attend my Bible Study, and myself went by one of our church member's house to pray for him, also my two sons. We were all standing in a circle, holding hands together, praying. I was praying, then all of a sudden everyone that was holding hands felt the power of the Holy Ghost; my mom started going down, and my husband had to sit her on a chair. The next day the two children asked me, Mrs. Coleman, what happened when you were praying with that man?

I explained to them that the Bible says in Acts 1:8—

But ye shall receive power after the Holy Ghost is come upon you: and ye shall be witnesses unto me both in Jerusalem, and in all Judea, and in Samaria, and unto the uttermost part of the earth.

One morning I was sitting in the teacher's room reading my Bible, and one of the teachers came in and asked me to pray for her, so we went in the bathroom, and she leaned over and asked me to pray for her back. Her spine was crooked. So I prayed for her, and I also told her that an evangelist was coming to town, and she should go and let him lay hands on her and pray too. So she went on Friday night. Then she came to school on Monday and called me back into the bathroom. She leaned over and told me to touch her back, and I did. She was healed. I was so happy for her. I told her, I am glad that you went Friday night. All of a sudden she said, Dorothy, I was healed before I went; when you prayed for me. I said, Praise God. Sometimes we think that God is using certain people, but that's not true.

Mark 16:17,18 says—*And these signs shall follow those who believe....they will lay hands on the sick, and they will recover.*

Another teacher asked me to pray for her leg. God healed her.

One morning I was in the class room, and this little girl was writing on the blackboard, and my leg was hurting. I did not say it out loud, but I said it to myself as I was passing by her. I said, in the name of Jesus be healed, and she fell back. She said, What happened? I did not tell her because she would not understand. But I knew what it was. It was the power of the Holy Spirit in me, and I was healed.

One day after work, I went over to a lady's house to pray for her because she was sick. And there was a man there that I had never seen before. Later I found out that he was a prophet. So I kept on saying to the lady, I wish that Doris were here, but he looked at me and said, It was not meant for her to be here. He told me to read John 9:4—*Jesus said, I must work the works of him that sent me, while it is day: the night cometh, when no man can work.*

In 1980 I received a phone call from my sister-in-law to come to the hospital and pray for my nephew who was three years old at the time. She said that she and my brother had been there for three days. The doctors kept running tests on her son, but they could not find what was wrong with him. I had taken my anointing oil with me, and I put some on my nephew. All of a sudden I felt very weak in my legs, like I was going to fall down. My mom and my husband were there, and my mom said, Al get up and let Dorothy sit down. Meanwhile my little nephew got up and walked all around the hospital with an IV in his arm. The doctors did not know what had happened. But we knew what happened. Jesus healed him. He is thirty years old today, has a beautiful wife and two little girls, and he loves the Lord very much.

I did not understand at first why I felt weak in my legs, but I do now. I asked my pastor, and he said read Luke 8:43-48— Woman having an issue of blood twelve years. She came behind Jesus, and touched the border of his garment and immediately she was healed.

And Jesus said, Somebody hath touched me: for I receive that virtue is gone out of me. So when I prayed for my nephew this is what happened to me, virtue went out of me into my little nephew. And this is why I was so weak. Praise God!

Another time I prayed for my brother, his leg was hurting real bad. I prayed for him, and Jesus healed him.

Al and I went over to Mrs. Scott's house, and there was a lady there who gave me a word of prophecy. She said I will meet some children who have been abused and molested, but when I put my arms around them and give them a hug, God is going to heal them.

One morning my friend and I went out witnessing. We met a lady who told us not to go on the other side of the street because it is really bad over there. The lady who was with me said, Dorothy, I don't think that we should go. And I told her we are going to go, because the Lord is going to take care of us. I told her you have to have faith. When I said that, a big wind came and started going round and round. I told my pastor what had happened, and he said to me, It was a <u>whirlwind</u>.

Hosea 8:7-- *For they have sown the wind, and they shall reap the <u>whirlwind</u>. It hath no stalk; the bud shall yield no meal; if so be it yield, the strangers shall swallow it up.*

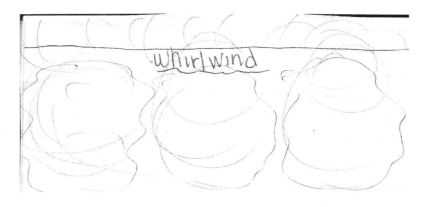

In 1982, my son, Mike, graduated from high school He played all three sports, baseball, football and basketball. He won many trophies and certificates, and received a scholarship award. He attended college for a year. He worked until the time he married on September 27, 2002. He then took a job driving a city bus in California. Mike and his wife never had children.

In 1985 my son, Jerry, graduated from high school. He also played all three sports, baseball, football and basketball. Jerry also won may trophies and certificates. He is the father of four beautiful children. He worked with his step-dad, and he was a very good father.

We all attended church, and the children went to Sunday School every Sunday.

A Visitation

One night I was in bed sleeping, and the Lord spoke to me. He whispered in my ear and told me to read Revelation 3:10. I got up out of bed, and I turned to Rev. 3:10. This is what it says: *Because thou hast kept the word of my patience I also will keep thee from the hour of temptation, which shall come upon all the world to try them that dwell upon the earth.*

2 Peter 2:9—*The Lord knoweth how to deliver the godly out of temptations.*

1 Corinthians 10:13—*There hath no temptation taken you but such as is common to man; but God is faithful, who will not suffer you to be tempted above that ye are able, but will with the temptation also make a way to escape, that you may be able to bear it.*

In 1991 we went to my husband's mother's funeral. On the way back there was a lady sitting next to me, but she did not talk very much until I took out the paper with the cross on it. She started to cry. She said I would like you to come to my church as soon as you can. My pastor has a word of prophesy for you. But I told her we could not make it because we had just left Al's mother's funeral, and he had caught a bad cold. So she asked me to lean over, and when I did, she told us to get out of California. When we got off the plane and went downstairs to get our bags, she was not there. When Al and I returned home we started asking ourselves questions. Why did she want us to go to her church? And why did she want us to get out of California? Al started to cry. He said Dorothy, I believe that lady was an angel. So we both cried, and we decided to go to the woman's church. No one there had ever heard of her.

Hebrews 13:2—*Be not forgetful to entertain strangers: for thereby some have entertained angels unawares.*

After we read this scripture we started making plans to move, and the Lord was with us. We told our boys what had happened. Jerry said he would move in the summer, and Mike said he would come later. But Jerry did visit us for Christmas. He had the children with him, and we had a great time.

So Al and I moved to Texas in 1993, and also my mom. We immediately looked for a church, and we found one where the people welcomed us right away. They called me and asked me to preach the Word because their pastor was out of town, and I said, You mean you want me to bring the Word? They said, Yes, we do. So I did, and they enjoyed the message very much. They asked me again and again. When my pastor was there he enjoyed it too. I had Bible Class with the young people every Wednesday. I also sang in the choir every Sunday. And they asked me to speak at the church for Missionary Day.

One Easter Sunday I was showing and telling about the cross that appeared on my paper, and when I had finished, this little girl came up next to say her Easter speech. But she would not at the time, and they kept trying to get her to say her speech, but she took off and ran over to the spot where I was showing the cross. She stopped and looked up with her arms up in the air as if she saw someone standing there. After that, she said her speech. My husband had filmed everything on camera, so when we got home, we were looking at it, and my mom said she saw Jesus or an angel standing next to me. Praise God!

I had a dream one night; I was walking down the street and some guys were following me. I looked up and saw an angel, and he smote them and they burned up.

Bad Guys Burning Up

Another time I was getting ready to go to church at night, my husband worked at night. I wanted to go so bad, but it started to rain, and I do not like to drive in the rain. So I went from one room to another looking out the window waiting for it to stop raining, but it kept on raining. Then all of a sudden the phone rang. It was a lady from our church.

She called to give me a word of prophesy. She said, Dorothy, the Lord told me to call and tell you to go to church, He is going to send His angels to take care of you. I looked out the window, and it had stopped raining, so I went to church.

Another time I was teaching Sunday School, my husband and I, and a little girl said, Mrs. Coleman I just wanted to tell you that there are two big angels standing next to you. I noticed earlier that she was talking to another little girl in our classroom, and she was pointing at me. I asked her later, Why were you talking to the little girl and pointing at me? And she said, I asked her, do you see the angels standing next to Mrs. Coleman? She said, No. So I asked my pastor why didn't one of the little girls see the angels standing next to me. He told me God did not mean for her to see them. It was meant for the other little girl to see them. So I asked my pastor, Why is it always the children seeing angels or Jesus standing next to me? And he said, Because children are innocent.

Looking out
the window

lady called from church,
and said, God told me to
call and tell you to go
on to church, God is going
to send his Angels.

My First Son's Tragic Death

Still in Texas, the missionary asked me to speak in church again. So all that week my mom and I went shopping for a white dress. We found one.

One Saturday evening my son, Jerry, called and told me that he and his dad, my ex-husband, went to buy a part to fix the toilet, and I noticed there was something in his throat, and he did not sound too good, so I asked if he was still eating healthy. He said, Yes, but before we hung up, he told me that he would be praying for me on Sunday, when I would speak on Missionary Day. He told me that he loved me, and I said that I loved him, and we hung up. I prayed and went to bed. I always prayed for my two sons, husband, myself, mom, friends and families.

The next morning (Sunday) my mom and I were getting ready to go to church; my husband had to work Saturday night, and got off Sunday morning at 7:00. He would come home, rest for three or four hours, then he would come up to the church to hear me speak. Meanwhile my mom and I went to church, and the pastor always asked if anyone would like to testify on how good the Lord is, and I was always the first one up. When I returned to my seat, someone came over to me and said, Your husband is outside wanting to speak to you. So I said to myself, I wonder why he is here now. I was expecting him in a little while. When I went outside the church I saw my husband sitting in the car, and he was crying. I said, What is the matter? And he said Jerry and his dad had been murdered. All I could do was start crying, and going down to the ground. Then all of a sudden I felt so much peace. Everyone came running out of the church. They ran over to pick me up. My mom came out, and when she found out what happened, she started crying too, and they took us home. My husband followed us. The pastor and some of the people came over to the house with us, and they all prayed for us. My husband and I had to go back to California and make arrangements for a funeral. But everyone in our church was so nice to us, they cooked food for us, and brought over flowers.

But before we left Texas, I prayed and I asked the Holy Spirit to find the people or person who did this. I said, Holy Spirit, you know where they are. You know every hiding place, house, etc. where they can be.

Arriving in California, we went to the police station where they let us talk to a detective. He said I am very sorry for your loss. While we were sitting there talking, the phone rang, and the detective said, Mr. and Mrs. Coleman, I'm sorry but we have to leave. That phone call was for us to pick up a guy in another state who was bragging about what he did, and someone called us right away. They said that he had on a wig. I had prayed that the Holy Spirit would find him, and he did. You can not hide from the Holy Spirit, he knows everything.

John 16:7,8,14—*Never the less I tell you the truth; It is expedient for you that I go away: for if I go not away, the Comforter will not come unto you; but if I depart, I will send him unto you.*

And when he is come, he will reprove the world of sin, and of righteousness, and of judgment:

He shall glorify me: for he shall receive of mine, and shall show it unto you.

In a few days my husband, my mom and myself went to the house where my son and first husband were murdered. We told my mom to stay downstairs while we went upstairs. There was blood all over the walls, bathroom, and the hallway where I use to walk up and down the hall praying all the time. Later one of his best friends came over, and he could not stop crying.

We learned that my son was coming home from work, and he and his girl friend stopped by the house so he could change clothes before going out to dinner.

My son went out in the garage and his girlfriend went on upstairs. As he was getting ready to let down the garage door two guys rushed under the door, hit my son on the head with something, and took him upstairs where they tied him up. His girlfriend told the detective later that my son's dad rang the doorbell, and the men said, You better let him in before he wakes up the whole neighborhood. So they pulled him in and tied him up.

The men searched the house looking for anything they could take with them. They wanted money, but there wasn't much, so they got upset and took out a knife. My son's dad said, Don't hurt them. They have their whole life ahead of them. When he said that, they cut his throat from one side to the other, then they cut my son's throat. Then they came after her, and one guy said, Do not kill her. But they cut her throat, leaving her for dead. She said that after they left, she got up, pulled the window back and jumped out. Always when my husband put up Christmas lights every year, he had a hard time opening that window. When she said she opened the window, I asked her, Did you have a hard time? She said No. She said the window opened right away. She said as she was jumping down, she felt someone put their arms around her waist, and she landed on her feet. She then ran next door full of blood. No one was home, so she ran around the corner where she passed out. Someone found her and took her to the hospital.

The detective told me when he went to the house that it was horrible, blood everywhere. The next time I spoke to her, I told her, I always prayed upstairs in the hallway close to the window, and you said when you jumped out of the window you felt arms around your waist, and you landed on the ground standing up.

I told her there were angels holding you up. Hebrews 1:14 —*Are they not all ministering spirits, sent forth to minister for*

29

them who shall be heirs of salvation?

Psalm 91:11—*For he shall give his angels charge over thee, to keep thee in all thy ways.*

Later she told me they had put bags over their heads. She told me the Lord showed her that while he had the bag over his head, he was praying, then he died.

About three or four weeks later, I asked the detective if I could go to the jail and minister to them and <u>forgive them</u>. He told me no, they were people off the street looking for someone to rob, and my son and his dad were the target. But he did not understand. St. Matthew 6:14,15 says — *For if you forgive men their trespasses, your heavenly Father will also forgive you:*

But if ye forgive not men their trespasses, neither will your Father forgive your trespasses.

Next, when I was in Texas I received a phone call from the district attorney asking me if I would like to have counseling. I told him, No thank you, Jesus is going to take care of me. And it's been over twenty-one years since as I write this book.

In Matthew 28:20—*lo, I am with you always, even unto the end of the world.*

In 1995, after the death of my son, my grandson was playing inside his tent one night. His mother told me he would stay up late at night and play with his toys, so one night he was up late, he looked outside the tent and he saw his dad and grandfather. His dad told him to come out of the tent, and he put his arms around him and told him that he loved him. Also his grandfather too. They both wore white robes.

My grandson was five years old. This is a letter that my grandson wrote, and he forgave them.

MY Father was Killed by some
guys who was jealous of what he
had. my father was Killed when
I was five years old, one of the
guys are in jail, the second guy
they got him, but there thinking about
what to do with him, they still didn't
find the third guy. But I forgive
the guys for what they did to my
dad. We all cryed when my dad had
died. but it made me mad for what
they had did to my dad. he was the
only farther I will ever have, he
spent alot of money on the things
that I needed. He was there when
we needed him. He love his Kids
very much and I Know that he didn't
want to go, but it was just his
time to go and be with the
Lord of Lord and the King of

One Christmas I was at my brother's house. We were talking and having a wonderful time, but I missed my son. He would always buy the Christmas tree every year.

When I went to bed, I started to cry. The Lord said, Dorothy, stop crying. In the morning you and Al go over to the house where your son and his dad were murdered. There will be lots of people there. I want you to pray for them.

The next morning I told my brother and sister-in-law what the Lord had told us. My two little nephews wanted to go too, so Al and I took them too. We were on the freeway, and I told Al to speed it up, because we lived about two hours from my brother's house.

Al said, Dorothy, the Lord told you that the people would be there, and they will. So when we arrived at the house, a lady opened the door, and I told her who we were. Meanwhile I was looking over her head trying to see if I could see any people. She asked us to come in. We went in.

I went upstairs where I had walked up and down the hallways praying days and nights. My two nephews followed me. I pointed to the floor and I said, Devil, you might have killed my son and his dad, but they are with Jesus.

2 Corinthians 5:8—*We are confidant, I say, and willing rather to be absent from the body, and to be present with the Lord.*

And when I said that, people started coming out of the bedrooms upstairs. We had four bedrooms upstairs. I was coming downstairs to the living room, and people were coming out of the kitchen to the living room. We were all standing in the room holding hands. I did not have to say much. I think that they knew we were coming. I prayed for them all, and they all asked Jesus to come into their hearts.

Miracles And Healing

One night my granddaughter was in bed with me after we had finished praying. I taught my grandchildren how it is important to pray just like I taught my two sons. I am teaching them the same way. Well, anyway, my granddaughter told me that night after we had finished praying, she said, Na Na, every night when you are sleeping, Jesus walks into the room. She pointed at the door then went on to say, He comes around to the side where you are sleeping, and then He puts his hand on your heart, and my dad and my grandfather are standing to the side with long white robes on.

And when she began to talk about the Holy Ghost, I began to cry. My mom was in the next room, and she heard me crying, and came to see what was wrong. So I told her what my granddaughter had just told me. Mom said, Dorothy, she was prophesying. When Jesus put His hand on your heart, He was healing your broken heart.

My granddaughter was three years old at the time, and today she is twenty-five, and still says the same thing.

Luke 4:18,19—Jesus said *"The Spirit of the Lord is upon me, because he hath anointed me to preach the gospel t the poor; he hath sent me to heal the brokenhearted, to preach deliverance to the captives, and recovering of sight to the blind, to set at liberty them that are bruised.*

To preach the acceptable year of the Lord.

Acts 2:17—And *it shall come to pass in the last days, saith God, I will pour out of my spirit upon all flesh: and your sons and your daughters shall prophesy.*

John 14:26—*But the Comforter, which is the Holy Ghost,*

whom the Father will send in my name, he shall teach you all things, and brings all things to our remembrance, whatsoever I have said unto you.

One night when I was sleeping I had a vision. I was walking in a field. I heard beautiful music, then I felt someone put their arm around my waist, it was not my husband. I woke up, and he was asleep. The Holy Spirit came to comfort me because my aunt had called me and told me that they found my cousin dead, and I had gone to sleep crying about my cousin. That is why the Holy Spirit came to comfort me.

John 14:16—*I will not leave you comfortless: I will come to you.*

We went to Alabama to visit Al's family. We ran across one of his friends we had not seen in awhile. We started talking and I asked him if he had accepted Jesus in his heart, and he said, No, so I asked him if he would like to. He said, Yes. So we prayed with him, and he accepted Jesus in his heart. About two months later, his wife called and said he was in a car with two other people. All of a sudden a big long white truck ran into them. My husband's friend is the only one who died. His wife told us that after we left Alabama, his life really changed, he would go in the bedroom, close the door, and pray every day. And she said, he would talk about my husband and I always. The Lord gave me this scripture:

Hebrews 3:7,8—*Where (*as the Holy Ghost saith, today if you will hear his voice) *Harden not your hearts, as in the provocation.*

Another time when I lived in Texas, I went to a women's revival for three days with two other women. Every morning I would get up, take a bath, put on my make-up, and get dressed. So one morning one of the ladies said, I will go downstairs and put our coats and Bibles there, so when you come down, you will have your seats. Meanwhile I was getting dressed, and the lady in the room with me said, I do not come to a revival to get all dressed-up. I told her, I just like to dress-up. And she said, Yes, but it doesn't make sense. I was getting ready to say something, but the Holy Spirit stopped me. By this time the other lady that had gone downstairs to save seats for us, came and said, Lets go.

Then as we were walking, there were a lot of people there, and this lady came out of nowhere and touched me on the back. She said, Missus, the Holy Spirit told me to tell you that he likes the way you co-ordinate your clothes. And that lady was standing right next to me, when she said that.

When I returned to Texas, one morning my husband and I were coming out of the house on our way to church. The lady next door said, I sure like the way you co-ordinate your clothes. So sometimes we have to be quiet and let the Holy Spirit speak.

John 15:26,27—*But when the Comforter is come, whom I will send unto you from the Father, even the Spirit of truth, which proceedeth from the Father, he shall testify of me.*

And ye also shall bear witness, because ye have been with me from the beginning.

Another time my husband and I went to California to see and pray for my cousin. She was in the hospital dying of cancer. Her mom was in the room with us, and as I was praying with my cousin she started to cry. She kept looking at me, and her mom said, What's the matter? But she didn't say anything. My husband told me he believed that she saw Jesus or an angel standing next to me.

My cousin passed away three years ago. Her mom called me at 1:00 in the morning and told me about her passing. I tried to go back to sleep, but when I did, I had a vision of my cousin: I was standing on the side of her bed, she looked up at me and said, Dorothy, I see Jesus, He is so beautiful.

When my husband and I went to California for my class reunion we were very excited to see everyone. We were taking pictures, so when it was time to eat, I put the camera on the table next to me. We were talking and having fun, and I went to reach for my camera, but it was not there. Everyone at the table looked everywhere for that camera. We looked under the table, on the next table across from us, and all around. Still, we could not find the camera. I went to the bathroom and I prayed. I asked the Lord to help me find that camera, because it had so many of my friends' pictures from the class reunion. I left the bathroom and went back to my table, and someone asked me, Dorothy, did you find your camera? I said, No. By that time someone said, Dorothy, is this your camera? I looked at it, and said, Yes, that's my camera. I said, Where did you find it? He said, On the table right in front of us. I said, We looked over there, it was not there. They did not understand why the camera was there, and no one saw it there before. That's easy, the angel of the Lord had put it there when I went into the bathroom to pray.

Psalm 34:7—*The angel of the Lord encampeth round about them that fear him, and delivereth them.*

We went to California another time and went shopping. I bought some earrings, so when we returned home I took out the earrings, and found that one of them was missing. My husband said, We are not going all the way back to California for one earring. And I said, No, that's too far. So we took everything out of the bags three or four times; still no earring. I prayed and said Lord, I sure do wish that I had that earring.

We put everything away and went to bed. The next morning my husband came in the room with the earring. He said it was in the living room lying on the floor where we took everything out of the bag. So I said, It was not there when we went to bed. He said, I know, but I believe the angel of the Lord put it there, because you wanted it so badly.

In 2002 many people in California called me, and told me that they had dreams about me with a long white robe on. I told them, Praise God. I have a scripture for that:

Revelation 19:7-9—*Let us be glad and rejoice, and give honour to him: for the marriage of the Lamb is come, and his wife hath made herself ready.*

And to her was granted that she should be arrayed in fine linen, clean and white: for the fine linen is the righteousness of saints.

And he saith unto me, Write, Blessed are they which are

*called unto the marriage supper of the Lamb. And he saith
unto me, These are the true sayings of God.*

When I lived in Texas for about twelve years, my husband and I would sometimes visit my aunt after church. One Sunday we went, and on arriving there, her daughter and son-in-law were visiting. Her son-in-law left and came back with lottery tickets. He gave his wife some, and kept some for himself. His wife was sitting at the table with me, and he went to sit on the couch next to my husband.

My cousin started scratching her ticket when all of a sudden she stopped and looked at me and said, Dorothy, what are you doing? My ticket was changing color. I said, I am not doing anything. Meanwhile her husband sitting on the couch said that his ticket was doing the same thing. He asked my husband, What kind of car are you driving so I will know next time to keep on going. He said, I am getting out of here, so he got up and left. My aunt called me the next day and told me that they never won any more.

I believe they felt the presence of God coming from God's anointed.

Another time when my husband and I lived in Texas, we would go and pray for the sick in people's homes. We would cook food and carry it to their home after church.

One Saturday my husband and I were fixing the food to take over to a lady's house after church on Sunday. I looked at my husband and told him, You know what, no one better mess with us, because we belong to God. So the next day we got up, got ready and went to church. When church was over, we went to the lady's house with her food, and were going to pray for her. As soon as we walked in, she looked at me and my husband and said, No one better not mess with you and your husband, you belong to God.

Psalm 105:14,15—*He suffered no man to do them wrong: yea, he reproved kings for their sakes;*

Saying, touch not mine anointed, and do my prophets no harm.

Another time in Texas I had a vision that my brother and Audrae Crouch would meet. I told my brother about it, and he said that he wants to meet him too, because he wants to ask him about music. My brother has a beautiful voice, and he use to sing.

When Al and I moved to Arizona we went to visit my brother and his family in California during the Christmas holidays. We all went shopping, then went back to my brother's house. Later that evening, his wife, myself and her daughter-in-law went to Walmart. Al, my brother, and his sons stayed home.

When we entered the store, guess who I saw. That's right, Audrae Crouch and his sister. I looked at my sister-in-law and said, There's Audrae Crouch and his sister. She looked at me, and said Who is that? And I said to her, Didn't my brother tell you about the vision that they would meet? She said, No. So I took her over to meet them. I introduced myself and my

38

sister-in-law, and I told him about the vision that he and my brother were to meet. My brother wants to know more about music. I did not know that I would be moving to Arizona, but God knew. We are about six hours from Arizona to California. Praise God, the Lord had it all set up. So he asked my sister-in-law, Where do you guys live? And she told him. He looked at her and said, You guys are right around the corner from my church. I would love for you to come. I would like to meet him, and he gave us some of his cards. When we returned home, I told my brother that we saw Audrae Crouch, and he wants to meet you, and I gave him one of the cards.

Sad to say my brother never got in touch with him, nor went to his church. He passed up his blessing. I believe if he had gone, his wife would have been healed of cancer. I believe it was not only the meeting of them getting together about the music, but I feel in my heart that he wanted them to come to the church so that he could pray for her. So we should obey God. She passed away January 7, 2017.

In 1985 the Lord woke me up in the middle of the night, told me to read Revelation 3:10. I jumped up, and my husband asked me, What is the matter? I had my Bible in my hand, and I told him the Lord wants me read Revelation 3:10. And this is what the Word says:

Revelation 3:10—Because thou has kept the word of my patience, I also will keep thee from the hour of temptation, which shall come upon all the world, to try them that dwell upon the earth.

1 Corinthians 10-13—There hath no temptation taken you but such as is common to man: but God is faithful, who will not suffer you to be tempted above that ye are able, but will with the temptation also make a way to escape, that ye may be able bear it.

Prophesy For Me

Father, I thank you today for Dorothy, and the anointing that's on her life. God has put a strong word in your mouth, and he wrapped it in grace and mercy.

But it's not a compromising word, it's a word of truth that God has put there. And there's a lot of times when people will say, Dorothy, you are too strong about this, or you are too hard about this. But the spirit of God is saying, Daughter, you know the truth, and the Lord says, you've been one, you won't mix truth with error because there's something in you that says you know the truth, and the truth will set you free. Now sometimes they don't want to know the truth. But God gives you the word to speak the truth. And he says that prophecy that's on the inside of you never wants to compromise, never wants to mix. Spirit of God says, Daughter, I am going to give you new authority in this hour, says the spirit of the Lord.

After the death of my son, when I was in Texas, this lady asked me to go to church with her, so I did. When we got there we started praising the lord, then all of a sudden there was a lady minister who started prophesying over me.

She said, Get ready for ministry. You are getting ready to come forth like never before. The oil is going to pour forth out of your hands, even when the enemy tried to torment you of the things that happened in the past, I hear the Lord say, I remove them this day. Healing. Virtuous.

And she went on to say, He's in the presence of his father. She was talking about my son, the the presence of his father.

Surely the righteous shall give thanks unto thy name: the

upright shall dwell in thy presence.

Let the oil of your anointing flow out of your life into others, and in the community. The oil is going to flow, and he is going to get you ready. Holy Ghost put boldness upon her that she may come forth. Thank you, Father.

This is what her husband prophesied over me: We prophesy according to faith. I see a vision, and God is saying that what they are seeing in the spirit, two of them are working together.

My daughter, I am going to give you wisdom. I am going to show you how to deal with the situation that you have been facing. You asked me for guidance, and you asked me to come out of the things that you have been asking to come out of, and now I am going to show you the path. I am going to prepare it for you, for you are going to know the things you didn't know before. And I am going to uncover, and I am going to show you, and begin to strengthen you and to bring you into your identity, to show and prove to you, as to who you are. And I am going to walk with you, walk you through the process where you have to go. And, my daughter, I am going to begin to show you a sign, and I am going to increase your faith so that you will know, and that you will have the authority and strength and boldness and make the decision you have to make. As you begin to put your foot down, even in the house, I am going to show you great and mighty things. I am going to back you one hundred percent. And my name is going to be with you. And you are going to have my strength, and I am going to steer you. You have desired the gifts of the Spirit to move in your life, and I am going to steer you toward that. And I am going to show others that there's more in you than they can ever imagine. And I am pouring my oil upon you. My anointing is going to begin to come up in you like you've never seen.

For I have already shown you <u>dreams</u> and <u>visions.</u>

We Move To Arizona

In march of 2005 the Lord sent us to Arizona. The first thing we did was to find a church. I was talking with my husband and I said to him, I wonder what will happen here. In California the Lord gave me many dreams and visions. Children saw Jesus standing next to me, Bible studies in our home, and much more. Of course when we moved to Texas, many things happened there too. Now we are in Arizona. We started working in the church right away with the Children's Sunday School. We had our own class; a beautiful class.

I remember one Sunday, I was teaching on the Holy Spirit, and I never sit down while I am teaching, but that morning the Lord told me to sit down. I sat down, and I notice this little boy kept looking under the table. So I asked him, Why are you looking under the table? And he said to me, There is fire all around you. I said, Praise God. That was the Holy Spirit. This was my first experience here in Arizona.

Prophesy in Church

One Sunday the pastor was preaching about David. All of a sudden he stopped and called my name. He said, Dorothy, God has given you the gift of healing. There have been people miraculously healed, and he said when people are sick I am going to send them to you. Pray for them. Use your gift that they might be healed. If you are sick, come to Dorothy, let her pray for you, because God is using her in the gift of healing, and I believe that revelation has always been there. And you have always said, God, I know that you are going to use me for something greater, and there's a day ahead that I am not going to be someone who is just going to sit in church. But God is going to use you for the supernatural to bring freedom to people's lives. And the days ahead, you are going to be incredible, because you are destined for greatness. You and Al both. We just call it out right now. In Jesus' name, that greatness will come out, that the gift of God will be released in you. We believe that we can call forth the gift of God. And we call forth the gift of God in this body, community, to you and to others, to be used for that gift of healing. We believe that because there is greatness in you, that God wants to call you out and to connect you with people, because we can see that gift in you. Greatness take place in your life.

In instructing His disciples regarding the coming of the Holy Spirit, Jesus said—*If I do not go away, the comforter will not come unto you; but if I depart, I will send him unto you. And when he is come, he will*:
(1) Convict men of the sin of unbelief.
(2) Convict men that Jesus in the righteousness of God.
(3) Convict men that the power of Satan has been broken.
(4) Regenerate the believer.
(5) Indwell the believer.
(6) Seal the believer.
(7) Baptize the believer.
(8) Infill the believer
(9) Empower the believer
(10) Lead the believer
(11) Administer spiritual gifts to the believer.

After we moved to Arizona I noticed one of my best friends had not called me for awhile, and I was concerned. We had known each other since we were twelve years old. I told my husband maybe she lost my address. Then one Sunday we went to Sunday evening service and there was a prophet there from Oklahoma City. He called for people to be prayed for, and when he got to my husband and me, he prayed for us and said that someone was looking for us. On the way home I kept saying, I wonder who could it be?

My son lived in California, and he drove the city bus. One Monday evening he called and said, Guess who got on the bus. I said, Who? He said, Gloria. I was so happy. The next day she called me and said she had lost my address and phone number. We have been in touch since then. Praise God, prophet and interpreter!

Matthew 10:41—*He that receiveth a prophet in the name of a prophet shall receive a prophet's reward;*

Deuteronomy 18:18—*I will raise them up a Prophet from among their brethren, like unto thee, and will put my words in his mouth; and he shall speak unto them all that I shall command him....*

Deuteronomy 18:19—*And it shall come to pass, that every soul, which will not hear that Prophet shall be destroyed from among the people.*

One Sunday a lady and her husband came to the altar for prayer. She said that she and her husband could not have any children, so Al and I prayed for them.

The next few months we saw them in the store with a baby boy sitting in the cart. He was about eight months old. She said, This is our little boy you guys prayed for a few months in the past. We said, Praise God.

The next year we saw them again in the market, and she was about to have another baby at that time. The next time we saw them in the store with another baby boy. We asked her if she wanted us to pray for her to have another one. She said, No, that's enough for now. But I thank God for my two sons, and for you guys for praying for us.

Another time Al and I were in the store again. We heard a lady telling another lady that she has cancer. When they had finished talking, I asked her was it all right if my husband and I could pray for her. She said, Yes. So we did. The next time we saw her, she told my husband and I that she was cancer free. I said, Praise God.

The next time we saw her, she told my husband and me that

she and her whole family started going to church. We saw her again, and she still says she is cancer free. This has been over five years ago. We give God all the praise and honor.

The Lord showed me in a night vision to read Ephesians.

Ephesians

Authorship, Date, and Place of Writing. Few critics have seriously denied Paul's authorship of this epistle. More attack has been leveled against the traditional date and place of writing, as well as against the traditional destination.

Ephesians is in the same chronological group as Paul's epistles as Colossians, Philemon, and Philippians, called collectively "The Prison Epistles," written during Paul's first Roman imprisonment. Paul evidently arrived in Rome in the spring of 61. The Acts speaks of his living two whole years in his own hired house (Acts 28:30), which would bring him to the spring of 63. He was probably released before the burning of Rome in 64. In Philippians he was expecting such release (1:19-26), a hope to which he refers also in Philemon 22. Ephesians, Colossians, and Philemon were dispatched at the same time by the same messengers. (Eph. 6:21, 22; Col. 4:7-9; Philem. 12, 23, 24), probably in the year 62.

Destination of the Epistle. Because the words in Ephesus (en Epheso) do not occur in the original handwriting of Codex Sinaiticus (Aleph) and Codex Vaticanus (B), two of the oldest extant manuscripts of the New Testament, some deny that this epistle was addressed to Ephesus. Another point of difficulty is the fact that an epistle from Laodicea is mentioned in Colossians 4:16, but there is no mention of Ephesus. Some believe that this epistle may have been a circular letter addressed to a number of different churches. It seems more likely, however, that a particular congregation was in view, and there is no strong reason for rejecting the traditional destination—Ephesus.

Contents of the Epistle. This epistle, along with Colossians, emphasizes the truth that the Church is the body in which Christ is the Head. While Paul had mentioned the same truth earlier, in Romans 12 and 1 Corinthians 12, he develops it more fully here. There is no higher point of revelation than is reached in this epistle which shows the believer as seated with Christ in the heavenlies, and exhorts him to live in accordance with this high calling. Actually the epistle falls into two main parts of three chapters each. In Ephesians 1-3 the apostle tells believers what they are in Christ; In Ephesians 4-6 he tells them what they are to do because they are in Christ.

Theological Significance. The theological insight and depth of this epistle are so great that some have considered to be the most profound work in the entire Bible. No book in all the Bible gives such a panorama of God's redemptive purpose— from before the foundation of the world to the consummation in the fullness of Christ. The breadth of the entire Biblical message is encompassed within the brief letter: God chose us in Christ before the foundation of the world; made us alive from sin by grace through faith in the Lord Jesus Christ; and, by breaking down the middle wall of partition between Jew and Gentile, male and female, bond and free, made us one new man in Christ, that we might grow up unto the measure of the stature of the fullness of Christ.

We are called to walk worthily of his calling in One Lord, One Faith, and one Baptism, keeping the unity of the Spirit in the bonds of peace. Such a summary of the vast reach of God's purpose is found nowhere else in all the Scriptures.

The theological themes stressed are these:

(1) Divine election. This most vigorously debated doctrine of Christianity is spelled out clearly in Ephesians 1:4--"God chose (the literal word is elected) us in Christ before the foundation of the world." God chose all who by faith would come into Christ. Election becomes effective when one comes into Christ, who was already chosen before the foundation of the world.

(2) Reconciliation. One of the great themes of Ephesians is that the barriers are broken down—first between man and

God, and then between man and his fellowman. Paul saw that Christ was the one who broke these barriers down. First, between Holy God and sinful man by becoming man. Second, between the races by bringing together in his body (the church) all the races as one new mankind! Third, between master and slave by placing us all on equal footing as servants of Jesus Christ. Fourth, Jesus broke the system where man dominated the woman, male and female were equal before Christ.

(3) The church. The dominant theme of Ephesians is the church as the body of Christ. He means that Christ functions in the world through the church, just as our human personalities function through our physical bodies.

Paul uses this body metaphor in several different ways. He calls Christ the "head of the body," indicating that Christ rules over and respects the church as the head directs the body. Paul even uses another metaphor: The church is the bride of Christ (Eph. 5), and she is to be faithful to him as the wife is faithful to her husband, surrendering her own life unto him.

2005-2010

December 1, 2005 I saw an angel in my dream, and my son Jerry was in my dream.

December 3, 2005 I had another dream. I was getting ready for a wedding. I had on a long white dress. My two sons were there. Also my husband and my mom were there.

Revelation 19:7-9—*Let us be glad and rejoice, and give honour to him: for the marriage of the lamb is come, and his wife hath made herself ready*

And to her was granted that she should be arrayed in fine linen, clean and white: for the fine linen is the righteousness of saints.

And he saith unto me, Write, Blessed are they which are called unto the marriage supper of the Lamb. And he saith unto These are the true sayings of God.

December 12, 2005 In my vision, I saw a big crown on my husband and myself.

July 11, 2006 Someone has been taking money from my account, so I asked the Holy Spirit to help me. I prayed about it, and the next morning when I awoke, I was on my way to get something out of the closet and the Holy Spirit spoke to me, telling me that it was an inside job. So I went to the bank and asked to speak to the manager. He came out, and I told him that someone has been taking money from my account. He said, How do you know? I told him my Father above told me. He looked at me like I was crazy, but when he checked my account he found that the money was missing. He said, I am sorry, Mrs. Coleman. I will have your money back in your account. Praise God, the Lord is so good.

John 14:17—*Even the spirit of truth; whom the world cannot receive, because it seeth him not, neither knoweth him: but ye know him; for he dwelleth within you, and shall be in you.*

July 24, 2007 One of my friends I have known for a long time, whom I sent a box in the mail, called and thanked me for the gift. She said when she opened the box, she felt the presence of God all over her house. I always pray when I am sending something to people; I lay my hands on whatever I am sending, and I ask the Lord to bless them.

May 29, 2008 Vision, Al and I were walking together then all of a sudden, we were both caught up together in Heaven.

1Thessalonians 4:16,17—*For the Lord himself shall descend from heaven with a shout, with the voice of the archangel, and with the trump of God: and the dead in Christ shall rise first:*

Then we which are alive and remain shall be caught up together with them in the clouds, to meet the Lord in the air: and so shall we ever be with the Lord.

August 15, 2010 I was teaching my Sunday school class how Jesus will separate the sheep from the goats.

Matthew 25:31-46—*When the Son of man shall come in his glory, and all the holy angels with him, then shall he sit upon the throne of his glory:*

And before him shall be gathered all nations: and he shall separate them one from another, as a shepherd divideth his sheep from the goats:

And he shall set the sheep on his right hand, but the goats on the left.

Then shall the King say unto them on the right hand, Come, ye blessed of my Father, inherit the kingdom prepared for you from the foundation of the world:

For I was an hungered, and ye gave me meat: I was thirsty, and ye gave me drink: I was a stranger, and ye took me in:

Naked, and ye clothed me: I was sick, and ye visited me: I was in prison, and ye came unto me.

Then shall the righteous answer him, saying, Lord when saw we thee an hungered, and fed thee? Or thirsty, and gave thee drink?

When saw we thee a stranger, and took thee in? Or naked, and clothed thee?

Or when saw we thee sick, or in prison, and came unto thee?

And the King shall answer and say unto them, Verily I say unto you, Inasmuch as ye have done it unto one of the least of these my brethren, ye have done it unto me.

Then shall he say also unto them on the left hand, Depart from me, ye cursed, into everlasting fire, prepared for the devil and his angels:

For I was an hungered, and ye gave me no meat: I was thirsty, and ye gave me no drink:

I was a stranger, and ye took me not in: naked, and ye clothed me not: sick, and in prison, and ye visited me not.

Then shall they also answer him, saying, Lord when saw we thee an hungered, or a thirst, or a stranger, or naked, or sick, or in prison, and did not minister unto thee?

Then shall he answer them, saying, Verily I say unto you, Inasmuch as ye did it not to one of the least of these, ye did it not to me.

And these shall go away into everlasting punishment: but

the righteous into life eternal.

I told the boys and girls how important it is to feed the hungry, give them something to drink. How Jesus said as a stranger ye took me in, naked, and ye clothed me, sick, and ye visited me, in prison, and ye came unto me. This is what Jesus wants all of us to do, and if we do not, He says in verse 46— And these shall go away into everlasting punishment.

So after church that day, Al and I went to the store. We were walking down the isle and talking when we met a lady who started singing a song to us: For I was hungered, and you gave me meat, I was thirsty, and you gave me drink, stranger, and you took me in. My eyes filled with tears. Al and I told her that we had just left church, and this is what we were teaching our Sunday school class. We were all so full of joy, because we knew that it was a word from the Lord.

I believe she was a prophet—A prophet is someone who delivers divine messages or interprets the divine will of God.

2011-2012

January 15, 2011 Al and I had started a Bible study in our home, and I prayed in my home for a mother who said her son was on drugs. The next time she came, she said that he was doing better.

January 17, 2011 Herb prophesied that God is going to use Al and myself in these last days, and the anointing will be strong in our lives, and God is going to take us places we have never been before, and miracles will happen.

February 23, 2011 I had a vision in my church. I saw little children and me singing and prophesying. Then I saw Jesus in a long white robe on the platform with a white veil over his face.

March 3, 2011 I dreamed I was laying hands on people, and they were falling out. This has come to pass. Praise God!

June 18, 2011 Dorothy spoke at the Women Aglow for forgiveness. I gave my testimony.

June 23, 2011 Summer Bible School. I was praying for children three years old. They accepted Jesus. The anointing was on me so strong. I almost fell out. People had me sit down.

October 26, 2011 At church I prayed for a little boy to be healed of tumors on his chest, and God healed him. His mother told me that he loves me, and that he never got close to people. She said that he told her there is a special bond between us forever. Praise God!

November 13, 2011 At 5 am, Sunday morning I awoke early. My husband and I teach Sunday School every Sunday, but this Sunday I awoke too soon, so I fell asleep again and had a vision. I heard the trumpet sound so loud, I work up. I said to my husband, Has Jesus come? He said, No, we would have gone with him. So when I went to church that morning I asked my Jewish friend, What did that vision mean? He told me that he believed that the Lord has more for me to do. I was really concerned, so I was reading the book *Blow The Trumpet in Zion*.

Warning of Judgment

1. Be a watchman
2. Get not wrapped up in the world
3. Look at distance at night and always
4. Be faithful; God has called us for this hour
5. Stay in his presence
6. Be strong
7. Get not caught up in the world
8. Always looking into the future to see what's coming.
9. We are chosen for this time.

Ezekiel 33:1-20

1 *Again the word of the Lord came unto me, saying,*

2 *Son of man, speak to the children of my people, and say unto them, When I bring the sword upon a land, if the people of the land take a man of their coasts, and set him for their watchman: Ez 3:11, 33:17*

3 *If when he seeth the sword come upon the land, he blow the trumpet, and warn the people; Neh 4:18, Hos 8:1*

4 *Then whosoever heareth the sound of the trumpet, and taketh not warning; if the sword come, and take him away, his blood shall be upon his own head. 2 Chr 25:16, Ez 18:33*

5 *He heard the sound of the trumpet, took not warning; his blood shall be upon him. But he that taketh warning shall deliver his soul. Ez 9:19-21, Heb 11:7*

6 *But if the watchman see the sword come, and blow not the trumpet, and the people be not warned; if the sword come, and take any person from among them, he is taken away in his iniquity; but his blood will I require at the watchman's hand. Ez 18:20, 24*

7 *So thou, O son of man, I have set thee a watchman unto the house of Israel; therefore thou shalt hear the word at my mouth, and warn them from me. Is 62:6, Jer 26:2*

8 *When I say unto the wicked, O wicked man thou shalt surely die; if thou dost not speak to warn the wicked from his way, that wicked man shall die in his iniquity; but his blood will I require at thine hand. Ez 18:4, 33:14*

9 *Nevertheless, if thou warn the wicket of his way to turn from it; if he do not turn from his way, he shall die in his iniquity; but thou hast delivered thy soul. Ez 3:19, 21*

10 *Therefore, O thou son of man, speak unto the house of Isreal; Thus ye speak, saying, If our transgressions and our sins be upon us, and we pine away in them, how should we then live? Lv 26:39, Is 49:14*

11 *Say unto them, As I live, saith the Lord God, I have no pleasure in the death of the wicked; but that the wicked turn*

from his way and live: turn ye, turn ye from your evil ways; and why did ye die, O house of Israel? Ez 18:23, 2 Peter 3:9

12 Therefore, thou son of man, say unto the children of thy people, The righteousness of the righteous shall not deliver him in the day of his transgression: as for the wickedness of the wicked, he shall not fall thereby in the day that he turneth from his wickedness; neither shall the righteous be able to live for his righteousness in the day that he sinneth. 2 Chr 7:14, Ez 18:21

13 When I shall say to the righteous that he shall surely live; if he trust in his own righteousness, and commit iniquity, all his righteousnesses shall not be remembered; but for his iniquity that he hath committed, he shall die for it. Ez 18:24, Heb 10:38

14 Again, when I say unto the wicked, Thou shalt surely die; if he turn from his sin, and do that which is lawful and right; Is 55:7, Jer 18:7, Ez 18:27

15 If the wicked restore the pledge, give again that he had robbed, walk in the statutes of life, without committing iniquity; he shall surely live, he shall not die. Ex 20:11, Lk 19:8

16 None of his sins that he hath committed shall be mentioned unto him: he hath done that which is lawful and right; he shall surely live. Ez 18:22

17 Yet the children of thy people say, The way of the Lord is not equal: but as for them, their way is not equal Ez 18:25, 29

18 When the righteous turneth from his righteousness, and committeth iniquity, he shall even die thereby. Ez 33:12, 13

19 But if the wicked turn from his wickedness, and do that which is lawful and right, he shall live thereby.

20 Yet ye say, The way of the Lord is not equal. O ye house of Israel, I will judge you every one after his ways. Ex 18:22

November 17, 2011 I was talking with a friend of ours in Texas. He use to travel with the Full Gospel ministries. He would go all around the world praying for people, and they were healed. The lord really did use him. He is eighty-seven years old now and he is still calling my husband and me.

November 17, 2011 John called me and told me that God gave him a vision of me, and that God is going to use me in these last days like Esther to speak up in such a time as this. Also God was showing him that there is a great cloud of witnesses around me.

November 20, 2011 At one of the churches the pastor was speaking on a subject that's not preached in many churches today. He said some might be offended. God gave me a word to tell him to keep preaching the Word, and the Lord will bless you. Some will leave, but if you remain faithful, God said, I will send more people. He said I receive it. Today the church has grown.

November 14, 2012 One night in a vision I saw the hands of Jesus. Luke 24:40—He shows his hands and feet.

December 9, 2012 One night in a vision I saw blood on the walls—blood of Jesus.

Luke 22:20—*This cup is the new testament in my blood, which is shed for you.*

1Peter 2:9—*But ye are a chosen generation a Royal priesthood. A peculiar people that ye should show forth the praises of him who hath called you out of the darkness into his marvelous light.*

The photo on the next page is of the royal crown that appeared on my chin as I was in the bathtub singing about Jesus.

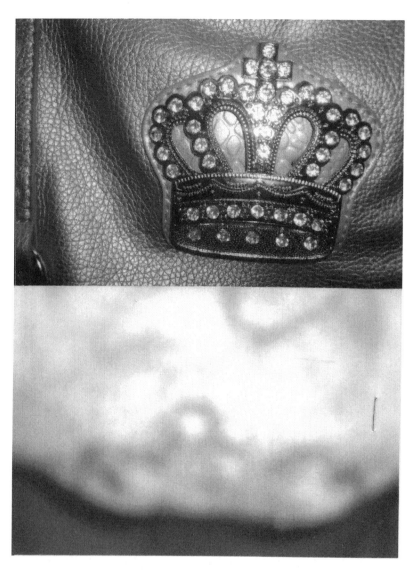

Royal Crown on my Chin

2013

February 25, 2013   Al and I went to have our taxes done at the AARP. There was a lady sitting next to me, and we started talking. She told me that her son was killed by gang members. I shared with her that my son was murdered; he was on his way to visit me. I told her that I am going to see my son again, because he is in Heaven. She told me that she was New Age, and that she sees and talks to her son all the time, and she did not want to have anything to do with the church. I told her that Jesus is with me always, and so is the Holy Ghost. And when I said that, she went to get up, and Al had to hold her up, she almost fell out. I believe the reason she almost fell out is because she was in the presence of God's children, and she felt the presence of the Holy Ghost.

John 16:8—And when he is come, he will reprove the world of sin.

March 1, 2013 I was praying with my son's friend in California and he told me he felt the presence of God, and he almost fell off the bed.

March 9, 2013 A lady I know who lives in California called and asked me to pray that they find the people that murdered someone she knew. I prayed and asked the Holy Ghost to find the person, and he did.

John 16:14—he shall glorify me: for he shall receive of mine, and shall shew it unto you.

March 17, 2013   I was in church; I prayed for a young man's house to sell. The next Sunday I went to church and his mother-in-law said the house sold the next day for $5,000 over.

March 23, 2013 I prayed for a husband's and wife's trailer to sell, and it did.

59

April 25, 2013 Al's sister was in the hospital. We prayed for her. That same night the Holy Spirit came into the room like a dove. He was right over my husband's head. The Holy Spirit came to comfort Al.

May 24, 2013 I prayed for a lady in our Bible study one night. She said she felt so much peace.

June 5, 2013 I had a vision of a black horse.

Revelation 6:5—*And when he had opened the third seal, I heard the third beast say, come and see. And I beheld, and lo a black horse; and he that sat on him had a pair of balances in his hand.*

And I heard a voice in the midst of the four beasts say, A measure of wheat for a penny, and three measures of barley for a penny; and see thou hurt not the oil and the wine.

July 22, 2013 I saw Jesus standing in the doorway of my bedroom in a vision.

Luke 24:36—*And as they thus spake, Jesus himself stood in the midst of them, and saith unto them, peace be unto you.*

August 1, 2013 At my Bible study one night there was a prophet, and he told me, Dorothy, I am sure that you already know it, but there are angels all over your home. Big ones, and they follow you every where you go. I told him, I am aware of them being around me. And he told me when I was praying with the people, they were standing next to me.

Hebrews 13:2—*Be not forgetful to entertain strangers: for thereby some have entertained angels unawares.*

August 4, 2013 I prayed for a lady at church. The doctor told her that she had a lump on her breast. She went to have an X-ray. When she went back to the doctor there was nothings there. Praise God!

August 28, 2013 My son, Mike, wrote my husband and me a beautiful letter:

Mr. and Mrs. Albert and Dorothy Coleman,
You are invited to a banquet. A family

60

reunion. The approximate time is very soon. The place is very near. The table is full, but the seats are half empty. We are waiting for more guests to arrive. As a child, I enjoyed taking care and loving you and your brother, and then when I got old, you took care of me. Someone up here keeps bragging about you and Al. He is saying that your work for him is not yet done, but soon it will be. My name is Florence Hubbard, I am your mother and I love you!!

Hey Mamma!

I guess you know who this is. Me and Roscoe are waiting for you too! How are all my kids dong? I even heard I was a grandfather.

I'm up here teasin' Flo, but she don't wear a wig no more.

Chip, Princess, Raider, Tinker are here too! Even Buster is here.

Listen, Mother, I've got a crown for you. I've got one for Al too! I hope t fits his big head. Someone up here keeps braggin' about ya. I call him Lord and Savior, but you call him Jesus.

The Banquet Table Is Set. You Are Invited

August 2013   Al received birthday wishes from Mike:

Happy, happy birthday 71!
Seems the older you get, the more God blesses you. God is good when? <u>All the time!!</u> You know me and this guy were talking about Jesus, and I told him that I think what actually killed Jesus, or the reason why he died was because he died of a broken heart. Obviously the physical pain was excruciating, but I believe he was heartbroken. Imagine the people he fed, healed, clothed, comforted. His disciples that he ate and slept with. The people today not

believing.

All these people turned their backs on him. He knew this, yet gave his life for all. Most of all God the Father had to turn away. His son had become the sponge that soaked the filth, the dirt, the sins of the world. "My God, my God why have you forsaken me?" And yet after all this, it was his mother at the foot of the cross.

I do believe in Christ, I am the fool that believes in God. But I will not pretend. The one thing I do know is that I love you and Al very much. You guys remind me of this Gospel song I like, I've decided to follow Jesus, though none go with me, still I will follow. No turning back, no turning back.

So keep on, keepin' on.
Love, Mike.

P.S. I love you, Happy Birthday 71. Al, I love you always. Stay healthy. When I see you, I will take you both shopping, and get something to eat. It's time I start taking care of you and Jr. you have worked hard all your lives taking care of Jerry and I. I still have a dream of buying you guys a mo bile home.

August 29, 2013 I woke up about 3:00 in the morning to

pray. The Lord always wakes me up every morning about that time.   So when I opened my eyes, I saw two little girls standing in the doorway of my bedroom. They were about eight and nine years old. They had on white robes. They were angels.

September 4, 2013   Al and I went on a mission trip to pray for Indian pastors.

October 5, 6, 2013   Another mission trip to pray for the Indian people, took clothes, etc.

Second Son's Death

November 4, 2013 The Lord woke me and told me to read 2 Timothy—perilous time. So I told my husband, and as we read 2 Timothy, Chapter 3, the telephone rang. It was my son's wife on the phone. I knew something had happened, because Al started to cry, and he gave me the phone. My son's wife told me that they had found Mike's body and the only way that they could identify it was by his teeth.

I really started crying. I birth my son into this world, I never thought the mailman would bring his ashes to me in a box. But through it all, the Lord has given me so much peace. I told my husband, I have no more sons. They are both dead. I really prayed the Jesus would give me the strength. This is why the Lord told me to read:

2 Timothy 3:13—*But evil men and seducers shall wax worse and worse, deceiving, and being deceived. But continue thou in the things which thou hast learned and hast been assured of. Knowing of whom thou hast leaned them.*

2 Timothy Chapter III
1 This know also, that in the last days perilous times shall come.

2 For men shall be lovers of their own selves, covetous, boasters, proud, blasphemers, disobedient to parents, unthankful, unholy,

3 Without natural affection, trucebreakers, false accusers, incontinent, fierce, despisers of those that are good,

4 Traitors, heady, highminded, lovers of pleasures more than lovers of God;

5 Having a form of godliness, but denying the power thereof: from such turn away.

6 For of this sort are they which creep into houses, and lead captive silly women laden with sins, led away with divers lusts,

7 Ever learning, and never able to come to the knowledge of the truth.

8 Now as Jannes and Jambres withstood Moses, so do these also resist the truth: men of corrupt minds, reprobate concerning the faith.

9 But they shall proceed no further: for their folly shall be manifest unto all men, as theirs also was.

10 But thou hast fully known my doctrine, manner of life, purpose, faith, longsuffering, charity, patience,

11 Persecutions, afflictions, which came unto me at Antioch, at Iconium, at Lystra; what persecutions I endured: but out of them all the Lord delivered me.

12 Yea, and all that will live godly in Christ Jesus shall suffer persecution.

13 But evil men and seducers shall wax worse and worse, deceiving, and being deceived.

14 But continue thou in the things which thou hast learned and hast been assured of, knowing of whom thou hast learned them;

15 And that from a child thou hast known the holy scriptures, which are able to make thee wise unto salvation through faith which is in Christ Jesus.

16 All scripture is given by inspiration of God, and is profitable for doctrine, for reproof, for correction, for instruction in righteousness:

17 That the man of God may be perfect, thoroughly furnished unto all good works.

November 5, 2013 (Vision) In the morning of November 5, I was lying in bed praying. I must have fallen asleep, then with my eyes wide open I saw the sepulcher where Jesus was buried. Then I saw an angel come out of the sepulcher, and go up into Heaven. He had on a long white robe.

The Resurrection

Mark 16: 5,6—*And entering into the sepulcher, they saw a young man sitting on the right side, clothed in a long white garment; and they were affrighted.*

And he said unto them, Be not affrighted; Ye seek Jesus of Nazareth, which was crucified; he is risen; he is not here: behold the place where they laid him.

The Ascension

Mark 16:19—*So then after the Lord had spoken unto them, he was received up into heaven, and sat on the right hand of God.*

Acts 1:10,11—*And while they looked steadfastly toward heaven as he went up, behold, two men stood by them in white apparel;*

Which also said, Ye men of Galilee, why stand ye gazing up into heaven? This same Jesus, which is taken up from you into heaven, shall so come in like manner as ye have seen him go into heaven.

Acts 2:16-17—*But this is that which was spoken by the prophet Joel:*

And it shall come to pass in the last days, saith God, I will pour out my spirit upon all flesh: and your sons and your daughters shall prophesy, and your young men shall see visions, and your old men shall dream dreams.

So the Lord is showing me that when Jesus came out of the sepulcher, he was risen, so the old devil might have killed Mike's body, but the Bible says to be absent from the body is to be present with the Lord.

When my Lord came out of the sepulcher, he was received up into Heaven. So the Lord is showing me that when I saw the angel, he was coming to get Mike and take him to Heaven, and he left his old body, which was rotten and decayed. But now he has a new body. Praise the Lord!

November 5, 2013   I had a vision of Mike at his aunt's house, and I passed by a lady and she fell out.

November 5, 2013   I had another vision, I saw the sepulcher and the cross appear on my chin. And I saw two angels.

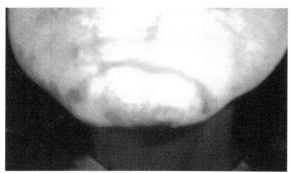

The Sepulcher On My Chin

November 6, 2013   In another vision where I saw a white rose, and it opened up. A white or pink rose means peaceful or carefree, free of troubles or anxiety.

November 6, 2013   I had my son cremated. His wife and I decided to do this because his body was so badly decomposed, even though I do not believe in cremation.

November 10, 2013 My husband and I had to teach Sunday School and I was sharing with the children some of the things about my son.

A little girl told me some things about my son. She told me some of the things I was talking about. She said that she had a bad dream about me, and that Jesus told her to pray for me. I put my arms around her and I thanked her. I was crying, and I told my husband, Out of the mouth of babes. Jesus sent this little girl to comfort me.

November 12, 2013 The Lord kept giving me visions. I saw Jesus going up to Heaven. Graves were open, people coming out. They had on white robes.

1Thessalonians 4:16-18—*For the Lord himself shall descend from heaven with a shout, with the voice of the*

archangel, and with the trump of God: and the dead in Christ
shall rise first.

17 Then we which are alive and remain shall be caught up
together with them in the clouds, to meet the Lord in the air:
and so shall we ever be with the Lord.

18 Wherefore comfort one another with these words.

November 13, 2013 My husband and I were eating breakfast
when we looked out the window and saw a cross in the sky.

The Cross In The Sky

November 19, 2013 The Lord Jesus filled my room with
beautiful angels. There were so many. They are so holy, so
pure, their light lit up the whole room. I could see their faces
shining. One came down to where Al was sleeping. He
looked so beautiful, then they all came around me.

I know they came to give me peace, because the next day
we had to go to the funeral home to make arrangement for
Mike.

November 20, 2013 Al and I had to go to the funeral home
to make arrangement for Mike's cremation. Even though I do

69

not believe in cremation, his wife said we should because his body was so badly decomposed. The night before we went, the Lord Jesus filled my room with beautiful angels. There were so many, they are so holy, so pure, that their light lit up the whole room. Angels are spirit beings created by God. They inhabit the spiritual world around us.

Psalm 34:7—*The angel of the Lord encampeth round about them that fear him, and delivereth them.*

Angels are ministers to God and to man—angels hear the voice of God and they obey Him. You do not walk alone through this life. There are angels who are delegated to assist, bless and protect you.

Psalm 91:11—*For he shall give his angels charge over thee, to keep thee in all thy ways.*

They have been sent to help Christians.

Hebrews 1:14—*Are they not all ministering spirits, sent forth to minister for them who shall be heirs of salvation?*

Not only do they have great power, but their appearance lights up the darkness so that midnight becomes like noontime. Angels deliver the righteousness to Heaven and death. When our spirits leave out bodies, an angel of God takes us to be with him forever. Worshiping angels is forbidden.

Colossians 2:18—*Let no man beguile you of your reward in a voluntary humility and worshiping of angels, intruding into those things which he hath not seen....*

The Bible says you should not worship angels, and angels do not want to be worshiped. They are never a savior, lord or god. They work for man; they are agents of God who bring to us the message that God wants fulfilled in our lives.

Sometimes an angel will appear and you will not realize it. God says that you should not forget to entertain strangers because it might be an angel that is trying to get close to you.

Who Receives Angel Service?

God's angels do not help hypocrites or people who do not truly love God. They cannot bless ignorance; therefore you must be wise and knowledgeable of the truth concerning angels. Angels have to bless spiritually. They pay attention to people who really want to do something for God.

Guardian angels remain close. If you fear God, you have an angel by your side to protect you.

Psalm 34:7—*The angel of the Lord encampeth round about them that fear Him, and delivereth them.*

When people see angels, they communicate this blessing to others. Obedience.

Romans 10:9—Romans 1:16—*For I am not ashamed of the gospel of Christ. For it is the power of God unto salvation to everyone that believeth.*

At the funeral home I asked the man if Al and I could go in back where they had Mike's body, because I wanted to read from the Bible the death of Lazarus.

John 11:21, 23, 24—*Martha said to Jesus, Lord if you had been here, my brother would not have died. Jesus said unto her, they brother shall rise again. Martha said unto him, I know that he shall rise again in the resurrection at the last day. Jesus said unto her, I am the resurrection, and the life: he that believeth in me, though he were dead, yet shall he live, and whosoever liveth and believeth in me shall never die.*

Jesus raises Lazarus from the the dead:

John 11:39—Roll the stone aside: Jesus told them. *Martha said Lord, by this time he stinketh, he has been dead for four days.*

V 40—*Jesus said unto her, Said I not unto thee, that, if thou wouldest believe, thou shouldest see the glory of God?*

So they rolled the stone aside. Then Jesus looked up to heaven and said, Father, thank you for hearing me. You always hear me, but I said it out loud for the sake of all these people standing here, so they will believe you sent me. Then Jesus shouted, Lazarus, come out. And Lazarus came out bound in grave clothes, his face wrapped in a head cloth. Jesus told them, Unwrap him and let him go!

The man at the funeral home told me that I could not go back there to read the Bible because it was against the beliefs of the other bodies back there, and I told him, What difference doe it make, they are all dead. So he told me we could go outside the building and read the scriptures, so we did.

If Jesus raised Mike from the dead or not, I still had the faith, because he said greater works we should do. People have been raised from the dead; maybe the Lord does not want Mike to come back to this evil.

December 1, 2013 After the death of my son, the Lord still sent angels to comfort me. I awoke on December 1, 2013 and I saw two little angels sitting in the doorway of my bedroom.

December 10, 2013 I saw more angels in my room. This time little children.

December 12, 2013 Again I say angels in my doorway. Little girls eight or ten years old.

December 15, 2013 I had a vision of <u>Hell</u>. Angels were throwing people into Hell. They were crying, but they could not get out.

Revelation 19:17-21—*And I saw an angel standing in the sun; and he cried with a loud voice, saying to all the fowls that fly in the midst of heaven, Come and gather yourselves together unto the supper of the great God.*

18- That ye may eat the flesh of kings, and the flesh of captains, and the flesh of mighty men, and the flesh of horses, and of them that sit on them, and the flesh of all men, both free and bond, both small and great.

19- And I saw the beast, and the kings of the earth, and their armies, gathered together to make war against him that sat on the horse, and against His army.

20- And the beast was taken, and with him the false prophet that wrought miracles before him, with which he deceived them that had received the mark of the best, and them that worshiped his image. These both were cast alive into a lake of fire burning with brimstone.

21- And the remnant were slain with the sword of Him that sat upon the horse, which sword proceeded out of His mouth; and all the fowls were filled with their flesh.

Revelation 20:2-15

2 And he laid hold on the dragon, that old serpent, which is the Devil, and Satan, and bound him a thousand years,

3 And cast him into the bottomless pit, and shut him up, and set a seal upon him, that he should deceive the nations no more, till the thousand years should be fulfilled: and after that he must be loosed a little season.

4 I saw thrones, and they sat upon them, and judgment was given unto them: and I saw the souls of them that were beheaded for the witness of Jesus, and for the word of God, and which had not worshiped the beast, neither his image, neither had received his mark upon their foreheads, or in their hands; and they lived and reigned with Christ a thousand years.

5 But the rest of the dead lived not again until the thousand years were finished. This is the first resurrection.

6 Blessed and holy is he that hath part in the first resurrection: on such the second death hath no power, but they shall be priests of God and of Christ, and shall reign with him a thousand years.

7 And when the thousand years are expired, Satan shall be loosed out of his prison,

8 And shall go out to deceive the nations which are in the four quarters of the earth, Gog and Magog, to gather them together to battle: the number of whom is as the sand of the sea.

9 And they went up on the breadth of the earth, and compassed the camp of the saints about, and the beloved city: and fire came down from God out of heaven, and devoured them.

10 And the devil that deceived them was cast into the lake of fire and brimstone, where the beast and the false prophet are, and shall be tormented day and night for ever and ever.

11 And I saw a great white throne, and him that sat on it, from whose face the earth and the heaven fled away; and there was found no place for them.

12 And I saw the dead, small and great, stand before God; and the books were opened: and another book was opened, which is the book of life: and the dead were judged out of those things which were written in the books, according to their works.

13 And the sea gave up the dead which were in it; and death and hell delivered up the dead which were in them: and they were judged every man according to their works.

14 And death and hell were cast into the lake of fire. This is the second death.

15 And whosoever was not found written in the book of life was cast into the lake of fire.

December 16 , 2013 I saw a big angel sitting in the doorway of my bedroom. He had on a long white robe.

2014

January 19, 2014 Again I saw angels in our room. Many were there.

Angels Everywhere In My Room

February 2, 2014 The Lord gave me another vision of my son Mike. He called me on the telephone and gave me a number to call him. He wanted to tell me something, but this dream is very personal. Sometimes the Lord would allow a person who has departed to appear in a dream to a loved one to bring comfort.

February 4, 2014 I had another vision. Mike was driving a white car. My husband and I were in the car.

Isaiah 1:18—*Though your sins be as scarlet, they shall be as white as snow.*

Psalm 51:7—*Purge me with hyssop, and I shall be clean: wash me, and I shall be whiter than snow.*

February 8, 2014 I saw in a vision two little girls standing in my doorway with Jesus. They all wore white robes.

February 9, 2014 I went on a mission trip. I had to testify.

February 14, 2014 Again in a vision I saw two little girls with Jesus in my room.

February 15, 2014 I saw in another vision, Jesus standing in the doorway of my bedroom. Angels and children were with Him. Then I saw a white cloud in our room.

Exodus 13:21—*And the Lord went before them by day in a pillar of a cloud.*

February 16, 17, 2014 I saw two little girls again standing in the doorway of my bedroom both nights; they were angels. I saw my son, he was about seven years old. They all came to comfort me. Praise God!

February 22, 2014 In a vision my husband and I went walking, and on the way home we saw my mom and my son, Mike, standing in front of the garage. My mom had on a red dress; she loved to wear red. We also saw Mike. He looked real good. His hair was short and curly. We all hugged and kissed each other. I said, Mike is this really you? He looked at me and smiled.

February 27, 2014 The Lord gave me another vision. This time I saw palm trees in my bedroom.

Psalm 92:12—*the righteous shall flourish like the palm tree: he shall grow like a cedar in Lebanon.*

Significance Of The Palm Tree:

The palm tree is a beautiful and useful branchless tree crowned with a tuft of lovely fan-shaped leaves. Israel encountered seventy palm trees at Elim (Exod. 15:27, Num. 33:9). The palm was a welcome sight to weary travelers for it always signified rest. Palm grows in Jerusalem. Jericho was called the city of palm trees. The palm tree was a common decorative motif in Solomon's temple (1 Kings 6:29, 7:36). Also Ezekiel's temple (Ez 40:16, 41:18). Palms were among the goodly trees used in the celebration of the Feast of The Tabernacles (Lev. 23:40). They form a beautiful poetical figure to describe the prosperity of the righteous (Psalm 92:12).

The straightness and beauty of the palm would naturally suggest giving its name to women: Thy stature is like a palm tree. The palm is a figure of the righteous enjoying their deserved prosperity (Psalm 92:12).

Palm branches are a symbol of victory (Rev. 7:9).-- *After this I beheld, and, lo, a great multitude, which no man could number of all nations, and kindreds, and people, and tongues, stood before the throne, and before the Lamb, clothed with white robes, and palms in their hands;*

The primitive church used the palm to express the triumph of the Christian over death through the resurrection; and on the tombs the palm is generally accompanied by the monogram of Christ, signifying that every victory of the Christians is due to this divine name and sign.

March 6, 2014 Again I saw angels in my bedroom, standing over by the clock.

March 8, 2014   I saw vapor of red smoke on the wall and clock.

March 20, 2014   In a vision I saw people in tribulation. There were so many people leaving their homes.

Matthew 24:21—*For then shall be great tribulation, such as was not since the beginning of the world to this time, no, nor ever shall be.*

April 2, 2014   In another vision I saw my late grandmother and my mom, they were young. Also Mike and Jerry. They were all sitting at the table.

May 7, 2014 In a vision I saw the Blood Moon on my cabin in the hallway.

May 22, 2014 A friend of mine called me and told me that she had a dream of me with a long white robe on

Revelation 19:8—*And to her was granted that she should be arrayed in fine linen, clean and white: for the fine linen is the righteousness of saints.*

May 30, 2014 In a dream I saw Mike. He was passing out

presents to my husband and myself.

June 6, 2014 One Friday night I was teaching Bible study in my home, and a lady said, my face was shining and there was light all around me.

June 7, 2014 Also another had a vision of my husband with a white robe on, and he was talking with people.

June 12, 2014 The Lord spoke to me in a vision to read The Virtuous Woman. (Proverbs 31:10-31)

July 21, 2014 In a vision I was talking to Jesus. I was walking around with him in the room. He was very tall, with a beautiful smile. I also saw my husband and my brother in the next room.

July 27, 2014 I was in a certain church, and they started singing this song, I Have Decided to Follow Jesus, no turning back, no turning back. I started crying and praising God, because my son, Mike, had written my husband and myself a letter back in August, 2013, how much this song reminded him of us. So when I heard that song, the spirit of God came upon me, and I was jumping up and really praising God, and this lady that was sitting next to me ran down to the other end. But all of a sudden I felt someone touch me on my shoulder, and I turned around, and there was a young man standing there with short blond hair and blue eyes. He had on a pretty white shirt. He looked at me and said, Missus, I love the way you praise the Lord. And one of the ministers got up and told the church that sometimes people get very emotional, but if only he knew what was in my heart that made me feel that way.

But anyway, my husband and I were called down to pray for people. We were standing in front of the congregation waiting for people to come for prayer. I noticed that I did not see the young man any place, and I asked my husband did he see him? And he said, No. So it was time for the service to be over and we got in the car and went home to have lunch before going to the nursing home to preach and pray for the people.

I never turn on the television when we come home to have

lunch, but the Holy Spirit had me turn it on. My husband and I were in the kitchen eating, and I turned on the TV to <u>Bible Prophesy</u>, and the minister was talking about angels.

Hebrews 13:2—*Be not forgetful to entertain strangers: for thereby some have entertained angels unawares.*

When I heard that, I started running all around the house. I told my husband that I knew he (the man in church) was an angel. He had come to comfort me. Praise the Lord!

September 8, 2014 In the room one night, I woke up and I saw smoke all around my husband while he was sleeping.

October 15, 2014 I saw people in a vision. They were running all over the place. Some were running and burning up.

November 23, 2014 On Sunday morning I had a vision of Hell. I saw people in the Lake of Fire. They were screaming, trying to get out, but they could not get out. In my vision I cried out to God, Please do not let my family go there. I woke up, turned on my right side, and went back to sleep. I saw the same thing again, and I started screaming and woke my husband. He said, What is the matter? I told him. So when I got up, I almost fell out, I was so weak. My husband asked me, Do you feel like going to church? I said, Yes. I am praying for my family and friends everyday. Hell is real. God does not want anyone to go there.

People In The Lake Of Fire

2015

January 1, 2015   I had another vision of my son. He was at my house helping me move the couch. When it was time for him to go, he turned around, looked at me and said, Mom, watch your neighbors. The Lord showed me that he was not only talking about my next door neighbors, but also the people that I am around.

Ephesians 6:8—*Praying always with all prayer and supplication in the Spirit, and watching there unto with all perseverance and supplication for all saints.*

Colossians 4:2—*Continue in prayer, and watch in the same with thanksgiving.*

January 8, 2015   I saw in a vision a lady wearing a long white wedding gown with a very long train

Isaiah 61:10—*I will greatly rejoice in the Lord, my soul shall be joyful in my God; for he hath clothed me with the garments of salvation, he hath covered me with the robe of righteousness, as a bridegroom decketh himself with ornaments, and as a bride adorneth herself with her jewels.*

Revelation 21:10—*And I John saw the holy city, new Jerusalem, coming down from God out of heaven, prepared as a bride adorned for her husband.*

January 14, 2015   I saw angels all in the house, little ones.

January 15, 2015   I saw Jerry standing on the balcony. He had on a white shirt. He looked real good. His hair was in a Jerry (Jhery) curl.

Isaiah 1:18—*Come now, and let us reason together, saith the Lord; though your sins be as scarlet, they shall be as white as snow: though they be red like crimson, they shall be as wool.*

Revelation 3:4—*Thou hast a few names even in Sardis which have not defiled their garment; and they shall walk with me in white: for they are worthy.*

February 12, 2015   In a vision I saw another big angel standing at my doorway.

March 11, 2015 I saw a lady in my room wearing a long white dress, I believe it was an angel.

March 22, 2015 I saw the Holy Spirit all around in my room, and angels were there.   Sometimes the Holy Spirit comes in like a wind; like a fresh breeze on a summer day. The joy of the Lord would fill me until I could contain no more.

March 31, 2015 Again there were angels in my room, and the Holy Spirit.

April 3, 2015 We went on Good Friday.   There were people from different churches. Al helped carry the cross.

April 4, 2015 I saw in a vision angels in our room, and there was smoke all around.   Jesus was standing in the doorway with a little girl.

April 19, 2015 I had a vision, my spirit came out of my body and I was looking down at a couple.   They went to a house. They were playing cards and playing Christian music. They said, I know we are doing the right thing. But the Lord showed me in the Spirit, you cannot serve God and the devil.

April 26, 2015 In a vision, Al and I were in a boat. We looked and saw Isis. They were coming toward us. A plane came and picked us up. Praise God!

April 26, 2015 God gave me a vision. Al and I were at a couple's house and they asked Al and me to go out on the back porch. There were two big dogs with us. It was real dark out there, very black, and there were lightning flashes, so we ran back inside.

I was so afraid, and they took us into another room. A lady came out where we were sitting at a table, and then she left. In my vision she was scary. I was so afraid. I awoke from my sleep, and Al was still sleeping. I did not wake him.

I prayed and prayed, and the Lord showed me something is

going on in that house. I felt the presence of the devil. I told Al, we will not be going over there any more. That devil is being exposed.

One day they called Al and me to come over to see their new house. As we walked through the house, I saw they had a deck and a porch just like in my vision.

May 6, 2015 I was at my cousin's house. In a vision I saw stairs, all white and holy.

Psalm 11:4—*The Lord is in his holy temple. The Lord's throne is in heaven.*

June 7, 2015 In a vision I saw my mom and many more people at my house. I went outside and looked up into the sky, and I saw the whole map of California. But only some places will have earth quakes.

June 12, 2015 Two of my friends were at my house sharing about the Lord when all of a sudden one said, Dorothy there is a cross in your hair. I said, Praise the Lord.

Acts 2:19—*And I will shew wonders in heaven and above, and signs in the earth beneath; blood, and fire, and vapour of smoke.*

June 25, 26, 27, 2015 Angels with Al and me. Holy Spirit in our room.

June 29, 2015 In a vision I saw Jesus in the sky. He had on a long white robe.

July 5, 2015 I had a vision of Paul and Jan wearing white. Jan came up to me, and talked with me and Al. She had her grandchildren with her.

July 7, 2015 A minister in Texas called me and said, Dorothy, if I could rewrite the Bible, I sure would put your name in it.

August 12, 2015 We were all at my niece's house and my other niece called and said that Aunt Dorothy, I had a vision of you. You had on a long white dress.

Revelation 19:8—*And to her was granted that she should be arrayed in fine linen, clean and white: for the fine linen is the righteousness of saints.*

August 14, 2015 In another vision I saw Jesus with a white robe on and light around his head. My husband saw in a vision the same night of Jesus wearing a white robe.

August 15, 2015 I saw people in a vision going up in the Rapture. A lot of white lights going up in the air.

1 Thessalonians 4:17—*Then we which are alive and remain shall be caught up together with them in the clouds, to meet the Lord in the air: and so shall we ever be with the Lord.*

September 2, 2015 On my birthday September 2, Al and I went to the store in Prescott looking for some plates and forks for our Bible Study. Al went one way, and I went the other. As I was standing looking at something, all of a sudden I turned around and saw a lady standing in back of me. I did not hear or see her when she came.

I had a cross on my purse, and she asked what did the cross mean to me? I told her the cross means everything to me. First of all my Lord and Savior died on the cross for me, and for the whole world. Also, he carried the cross, and was beaten. So this is why I am carrying this purse to let the whole world know that I love Jesus very much, and that I am not ashamed of him. This is why I also wear this cross around my neck and on my finger. She asked me what church do you attend? I told her the church I attend, and asked her would she like to come and visit us? And she said, yes; but I told her it does not matter what church we attend. The church cannot save us, only Jesus. She looked at me and smiled with tears in her eyes, then she left.

Al came up and we went looking for the plates, and it hit me all of a sudden, and I told Al go up front and see if you see that lady. He went one way and I went the other way, but we did not see her. I told him, look at that long line; she could not have gone through it that fast.

I told him, That was an angel, and I started to cry.

Hebrews 13:2—*Be not forgetful to entertain strangers: for they by some have entertained angels unawares.*

September 20, 2015 In a vision I saw an airplane falling from Heaven, and fire coming down from Heaven.

October 19, 2015 I had a vision at 3:00 in the morning. I was praying. I was telling the Lord Jesus how much I love him and the Holy Spirit. They are so good to Al and myself. We are so thankful to be called your children.

II Thessalonians 2:13—*But we are bond to give thanks always to God for you brethern beloved of the Lord, because God hath from the beginning chosen you to salvation through sanctification of the Spirit and belief of the truth.*

1 Thessalonians 1:4—*Knowing, brethren beloved, your election of God.*

Colossians 3:12—*Put on therefore, as the elect of God, holy and beloved, bowels of mercies, kindness, humbleness of mind, meekness, longsuffering:*

I started to cry thinking about the Lord, and how he has brought us through so much. And I was also saying to the Lord how much I miss mom, Mike and Jerry, and that I will be glad when we all meet together soon in Heaven, and to see his beautiful face.

I started praying in the spirit (tongues), and the Lord told me that he loves Al and me very much, and that he has work for us to do.

So I went to sleep. I had a vision: Al and I were in church. I do not know which church. It was a Holy Ghost filled church. The people were so happy. I was at a table with a couple, and they had a baby. I got up and went out the door. I was upstairs looking down, and I saw my brother. He looked up at me and said, I saw you here before, and he kept walking.

There was a lady standing in back of me. I turned around and hugged her. I told her that Jesus loved her very much, and so do I.

I said good bye, and went downstairs looking for Al. I could not find him. I went down the street looking for him. As I was walking down the street, on each side of the road I saw some weird looking guys. They looked like they were from Hell. They came after me. I did not run, I was not afraid.

I was walking with my head up looking toward Heaven. And I was saying, _Yea, though I walk through the valley of the shadow of death, I will fear no evil: for thou art with me; thy rod and they staff they comfort me._ (Psalm 23:4)

Psalm 3:6—_I will not be afraid of ten thousands of people that have set themselves against me round about._

Isaiah 43:2—_When thou passest through the waters, I will be with thee; and through the rivers, they shall not overflow thee: when thou walkest through the fire, thou shalt not be burned; neither shall the flame kindle upon thee._

Psalm 66:10, 12—For thou, O God, hast proved us: thou hast tried us, as silver is tried. V 12—Thou hast caused men to ride over our heads; we went through fire and through water: but thou broughtest us out into a wealthy place.

Psalm 91:3—_Surely he shall deliver thee from the snare of the fowler, and from the noisome pestilence._ (raging) (epidemic)

Deuteronomy 31:6—_Be strong and of good courage, fear not, nor be afraid of them: for the lord thy God, he it is that doth go with thee; he will not fail thee, nor forsake thee._

Deuteronomy 1:29—_Then I said unto you, dread not, neither be afraid of them._

Daniel 3:25—_He answered and said, lo, I see four men loose, walking in the midst of the fire, and they have no hurt: And the form of the fourth is like the Son of God._

Then I saw myself going up into Heaven. I saw beautiful lights, shining all around me. I was going so fast, I said Lord, I can't go right now, I have to take care of Al, and we have work to do. I woke up. I was crying. I did not want to wake up Al.

I went to get up, and I fell back on the bed. The power of God was so great. I finally made it to the living room where I went down on my knees. Still I could not get up. It was 5:00 in the morning and I went to sleep on the floor, and stayed there for about thirty minutes.

I got up and got on the couch and slept until 8:00. Al came in and asked, What are you doing in here? I told him what had happened. He took me by the hand and led me to the bedroom. I was so weak; the power of God was all over me.

I remained weak until Tuesday evening.

I Was Going Up Into Heaven

Psalm 11:4—*The Lord is in his holy temple. The Lord's throne is in heaven: his eyes behold, his eyelids try the children of men.*

Revelation 22:16—*I Jesus have sent mine angel to testify unto you these things in the churches. I am the root and the offspring of David, and the bright and morning star.*

Revelation 21:23—*And the city had no need of the sun, neither of the moon, to shine in it: for the glory of God did lighten it, and the Lamb is the light thereof.* (illuminate)

Light-up gold or colored decorations, glorify, emitting or reflecting much light; of brilliant color; splendid or glorious. Jesus is the light of the world.

October 29, 2015 In a vision I saw a <u>white horse</u>, and he that sat upon him was called faithful and true, and in righteousness he doth judge and make war.

His eyes were as a flame of fire, and on his head were many crowns; and he had a name written, that no man knew, but he himself.

And he was clothed with a vesture dipped in blood: and his name is called the Word of God.

And the armies which were in heaven followed him upon the white horse, clothed in fine linen, white and clean.

And out of his mouth goeth a sharp sword, that with it he should smite the nations: and he shall rule them with a rod of iron: and he treadeth the winepress of the fierceness and wrath of Almighty God.

And he hath on his vesture and on his thigh a name written KING OF KING, AND LORD OF LORDS.

October 31, 2015 On October 31 I saw angels in our bedroom.

November 3, 2015 On November 3 I saw the Holy Spirit in our room.

November 4, 2015 On November 4 I saw two angels standing in the doorway of our bedroom, a lady and a man.

Psalm 91
The Security Of The Godly

On November 15, 2015, my pastor was preaching on Psalm 91. He was saying, We are living in dangerous times, but we are not to be afraid, for the terror by night, and for us to put our trust in the Lord. We should not fear the pestilence that walketh in the darkness, nor for the destruction that wasteth at noonday.

Only with thine eyes shalt thou behold and see the reward of the wicked. There shall no evil befall thee, neither shall any plague come nigh thy dwelling. For he shall give his angels charge over thee, to keep thee in all thy ways. Because he hath set his love upon me, therefore will I deliver him:

Psalm 91:14—*I will set him on high, because he hath known my name.*

Psalm 9:10—*And they that know thy name will put their trust in thee for thou, Lord hast not forsaken them that seek thee.*

Psalm 91:15, 16—*He shall call upon me, and I will answer him: I will be with him in trouble; I will deliver him, and honour him.*

With long life will I satisfy him, and show him my salvation.

November 22, 2015 (vision) Al and I were in first A.M.E. Church. We were walking together in the church when all of a sudden we were apart. I went looking for him because the church was so big. I went upstairs, he was not there. I went all over, and I could not find him. I was so tired that I went to sit down, and I saw a young man on his phone sitting down at the table with me. We talked, and I told him that I could not find my husband. He said, I will help you find him. So we went out and started walking; it was in a big mall this time.

Far ahead of us I could see Mike coming toward us. I told the young man, I see my son coming toward us. And when he got closer, it was him. He looked so good; I ran to hug him. His hair was cut on the side, and some on the top, and he was dressed real nice. He was so happy. He carried a bag in his hand, and the guitar he loved to play.

I told the guy, Touch him. Is this really for real? Is he alive? The guy touched him, and said, He is for real all right. I was so happy that I kept touching him and rubbing his arms. I kept rubbing and pinching him to see if he was for real.

When I woke up I started to cry. I asked the Lord, Lord if it was real. I touched him, and the Lord said, But the next time it will be for real—real soon. My daughter, Mike is doing just fine. He is in one of the most beautiful places. I am taking care of him, and no one will ever be able to hurt him any more. Yes, when you touched him, he was for real, but when you really see him, it will be for real, and all of your family will be together real soon forever.

I am going to take care of you and Al, because I have work for you to do. So stay strong. I am coming soon. I love you very much.

December 19, 2015 At 7:00 in the morning, I was praying. I fell asleep for a short moment, and I had a vision. I dreamed that Al and I were at our church. We were all in a room together praising the Lord. We began putting some things in boxes when our pastor came inside from cutting the grass outside. Someone said, It's getting real dark outside. We looked out the window, and it did look very bad. The pastor told everyone to pray in the Holy Ghost and trust God.

We were in a tornado. It was very bad. I found myself in the corner of the kitchen praying, and we were all together flowing down the river. It was like we were all in a big bubble on top of a lot of debris flowing down the river, but it did not touch us. We were all safe, going down the river. This vision reminded me of when God told Noah to build an ark, and all of his family was saved.

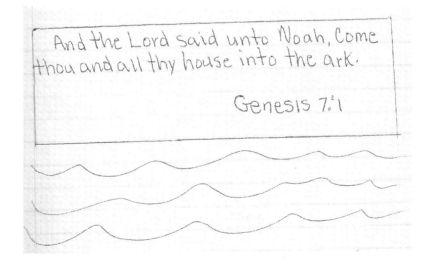

And the Lord said unto Noah, Come thou and all thy house into the ark.

Genesis 7:1

I thank God for our pastor for teaching us the word of God, and telling us to pray in the Holy Ghost. The Holy Ghost will lead and guide us in all truth.

Trust in the Lord always. Live a godly life, fear God, walk with the Lord daily, and he will direct our path. But the wicked he will (eliminate) get rid of, remove, ignore.

2016

February 10, 2016 I had a vision of angels blowing the trumpet. I saw people coming out of the graves to meet the Lord in the air. I saw lots of bright lights.

1 Corinthians 15:51-53—*Behold, I shew you a mystery; we shall not all sleep, but we shall all be changed.*

In a moment, in the twinkling of an eye, at the last trump: for the trumpet shall sound, and the dead shall be raised incorruptible, and we shall be changed.

For this corruptible must put on incorruption, and this mortal must put on immortality .

The Rapture When The Angel Blows The Trumpet

February 23, 2016 My back was in pain, and I said Lord Jesus, I am hurting so bad. My husband and I saw a cross in the sky.

The Cross And Clouds In The Sky

February 24, 2016 In a vision I saw a lamb in the corner of my bedroom. Then I saw angels in the room.

John 1:29, 36—*The day John seeth Jesus coming onto him, and saith, Behold the Lamb of God, which taketh away the sin of the world.*

And looking upon Jesus as he walked, he saith, Behold the Lamb of God.

February 28, 2016 I went to the altar for prayer.

Back in January our church had a tent revival. We had a wonderful time; people were healed and saved.

So when it was time to leave, it was very cold outside. About a couple of days later I felt a real bad pain in my left shoulder. The pain was so bad I could hardly raise my arm. I started to pray right away, but the pain got worse and worse.

When Sunday came, I said, Jesus I am going to trust you. I prayed every day like I always do, and read healing scriptures. Jesus, you said in your word that I am healed, and I believe it. I am standing on your word.

On my way to church, I said, Lord I know you have a word for me today. As we were singing praise and worship, the pastor said, There is someone on the left side of the church being healed; just move your arm around, and I said, Lord, that's me!

When I left the church, Al and I went home, ate lunch, and later we took a nap. While sleeping, I had a vision. I saw my son, Mike, in church with a microphone in his hand. He sure did look good. He was talking about me, about how much faith I have in God.

He said, When Jerry and I were little children, my mom and dad lived for God every day. They walked with God, they trusted God. And he started to say something about the Pharisees, but the pastor took the microphone, and Mike smiled and said, Thank you, pastor, for allowing me to speak. There was a lady sitting next to me on one side, and Al on the other side. She was really crying. This is the scripture the Lord gave me to read:

Hebrews 12:1,2—*Wherefore seeing we also are compassed about with so great a cloud of witnesses, let us lay aside every weight, and the sin which doth so easily beset us, and let us run with patience the race that is set before us.*

Looking unto Jesus the author and finisher of our faith; who for the joy that was set before him endured the cross, despising the shame, and is set down at the right hand of the throne of God.

March 25, 1964 Mike was born on this day. Also Good Friday was on Friday, the twenty-fifth of March.

March 27, 2016 On March 27th, Easter Sunday, God gave me a vision.

I was coming out of my house. I saw Mom, Jerry, and Mike coming out of my house with so many people. They sure did look good, happy and well dressed.

I looked up the street, and I saw Mike coming up the street. He sure did look good. His hair one one side was a light color, like blond.

We were all laughing and hugging each other. Al was watching the basketball game one night, and one of the guys that was on the team had his hair like I saw in the vision. These are the scriptures the Lord gave me about Mike:

Galatians 2:20—*I am crucified with Christ: nevertheless I live; yet not I, but Christ liveth in me: and the life which I now live in the flesh I live by the faith of the Son of God, who loved me, and gave himself for me.*

Romans 6:6-8—*Knowing this, that our old man is crucified*

with him, that the body of sin might be destroyed, that hence forth we should not serve sin.

For he that is dead is freed from sin.

Now if we be dead with Christ, we believe that we shall also live with him.

Revelation 21:4,5—(The New Jerusalem) And God shall wipe away all tears from their eyes; and there shall be no more death, neither sorrow, nor crying, neither shall there be any more pain: for the former things are passed away.

And he that sat upon the throne said, Behold, I make all things new.

May 8, 2016—Mothers' Day I had a dream about my two sons, Mike and Jerry. They were both at home. They went outside to play, then both came back inside.

I had this dream on Saturday night. The next morning was Sunday, Mothers' Day. Al and I got up and went to church. My pastor stood at the door handing out flowers to the women for Mothers' Day. (White Roses)

When I went up to him, he first gave me one, then he said, I need to give you two. So he gave me two white flowers. There was a lady standing near, and she said, Why did I only get one? The pastor did not say anything. I went inside the church and we started singing praises and worship, and the Holy Spirit spoke to me and said, One white flower for Mike, and the other white flower is for Jerry; my two sons who are no longer with me. I said, Thank you, Jesus. When the service was over, I went up to the pastor, and told him about what had happened in the service when the Holy Ghost spoke to me, and told me that the two flowers were for my two sons. He looked at me and said, the Holy Ghost told him to give me two flowers. Praise the Lord!

White roses mean peaceful or a carefree time.

May 26, 2016 God gave me a beautiful vision of my cousin Sharon who passed away four years ago. I saw in my vision that she had a lot of beautiful jewels in her room; all different colors.

Revelation 21:18,21—*And the building of the wall of it was jasper: and the city was pure gold, like unto clear glass. And the foundations of the wall of the city were garnished with all manner of precious stones.*

And the twelve gates were twelve pearls: every several gate was of one pearl: and the street of the city was pure gold, as it were transparent glass.

I had another vision of my son Jerry carrying a tall beautiful glass.

One Sunday before Sunday School started, this little guy in our class told me that his mom was on her knees praying. He looked over in the corner of the room and he saw Jesus, and Jesus had in his hand a box full of jewels. Praise the Lord!

A jewel is a precious stone: gem. A bit of gem, crystal, glass, etc.

July 29, 2016 In a vision I saw people running. There was fire all over the place.

August 11, 2016 In California there was a fire and eighty people lost their homes.

September 7, 2016 In my vision I saw three children going up in the rapture. I believe that they were my grandchildren. I had spoken to one of them the day before.

October 6, 2016 I had an open vision. I was talking to Al with my eyes closed, and I saw Matthew hurricane. I saw lots of water.

October 19, 2016 In another vision I saw my mom, Mike, and Jerry. I saw a white flower. The flower of such a shrub, usually having five sepals and a wide range of colors, principally white, yellow, pink, or red.

Rose: means past tense of rise. To move upward; go from a lower to a higher position. To appear above the horizon: said of heavenly bodies.

1 Thessalonians 4:13-17—*But I would not have you to be ignorant, brethern, concerning them which are asleep, that ye sorrow not, even as others which have no hope.*

For if we believe that Jesus died and rose again, even so them also which sleep in Jesus will God bring with him.

For this we say unto you by the word of the Lord, that we which are alive and remain unto the coming of the Lord shall not prevent them which are asleep.

For the Lord himself shall descend from heaven with a shout, with the voice of the archangel, and with the trump of God: and the dead in Christ shall rise first.

Then we which are alive and remain shall be caught up together with them in the clouds, to meet the Lord in the air: and so shall we ever be with the Lord.

Wherefore comfort one another with these words.

October 22, 2016 I dreamed about my mother. She told me not to tell people about my dreams and visions. Jesus said in Matthew 7:6 *Give not that which is holy unto the dogs, neither cast ye your pearls before swine, lest they trample them under their feet, and turn again and rend you.*

2017

February 2, 2017 The Lord keeps giving me dreams and visions of my mom, Mike and Jerry. I dreamed we were all together in a house talking and having fun together. I believe that one day all of our families will be together.

I Corinthians 15:51—*Behold I shew you a mystery; we shall not all sleep, but we shall all be changed. V. 52 -In a moment, in the twinkling of an eye, at the last trump:*

March 27, 2017 In a vision I looked up in the sky, and I saw angels.

This little boy took my pen, I got it back. It says preshaped today. It means Jesus could come any time. Then I smell a sweet fragrance in my room. (A pleasant scent; sweet odor)

April 8, 2017 Women's Breakfast. I spoke on Forgiveness.

Matthew 6:14, 15—*Jesus said, for if ye forgive men their trespasses, your heavenly Father will also forgive you:*

But if ye forgive not men their trespasses, neither will your Father forgive your trespasses.

April 9, 2017 I went to church on Sunday, and went to the altar. My pastor prayed for me, and he said, The glory of God is all over me.

April 16, 2017 The next Sunday is Easter. I met a lady at the nursing home, and I prayed for her mother. She asked me if I could go to her mom's house to pray for her, so Al and I went to her mother's house to pray. As I prayed for her, her daughter started to cry. Praise God!

May 9, 2017 On May ninth, I had another vision. I saw Hell and lots of fire. No one was in it.

Revelation 20:14, 15—And death and Hell were cast into the

lake of fire. This is the second death.

And whosoever was not found written in the book of life was cast into the lake of <u>fire</u>.

May 11, 2017 I woke up and saw on the wall red <u>flames</u>. To light up or burn as if on fire: flash.

Isaiah 5:24—*Therefore as the <u>fire</u> devoureth the stubble, and the <u>flame</u> consumeth the chaff, so their root shall be as rottenness, and their blossom shall go up as dust: because they have cast away the law of the Lord of hosts, and despised the word of the Holy One of Israel.*

May 21, 2017 In a vision Jesus was giving me a vase with red and white flowers in it.

A peaceful or carefree time. Not in a state of war, riot, or commotion, undisturbed.

Carefree—free of troubles, or anxiety.

June 1, 2 2017 In a vision I saw my mom, Mike and Jerry. We were all in the house together, laughing and having so much fun together.

November 30, 2017 I saw writing on the wall and I saw Jesus' face. He was letting me know to get back to writing my book.

December 10, 2017 Writing appeared on my wall—work on book.

The New Jerusalem

Revelation 21—*And I saw a new heaven and a new earth: for the first heaven and the first earth were passed away; and there was no more sea.*

And I, John, saw the holy city, new Jerusalem, coming down from God out of heaven, prepared as a bride adorned for her husband.

And God shall wipe away all tears from their eyes; and there shall be no more death, neither sorrow, nor crying, neither shall there be any more pain: for the former things are passed away.

And he that sat upon the throne said, Behold, I make all things new. And he said unto me, Write: for these words are true and faithful.

And he said unto me, It is done. I am Alpha and Omega, the beginning and the end. I will give unto him that is athirst the fountain of water of life freely.

He that overcometh shall inherit all things; and I will be his God, and he shall be my son.

My sister-in-law passed last year in January. My nephew called me and told me before she passed, she had a vision of Jesus, and Jesus showed her my two sons, and Mom, and more family walking on the streets of gold. (Praise God)

John 3:3: *Verily, verily, I say unto thee, Except a man be born again, he cannot see the kingdom of God.*

John 3:16: *For God so loved the world, that he gave his only begotten Son, that whosoever believeth in him should not perish, but have everlasting life.*

For all my readers who have not accepted Jesus as their Savior I would like you to pray this prayer with me so that you will become a born-again Christian: <u>Dear Lord Jesus, I know that I am a sinner. Thank you for dying on the cross and shedding your blood for me to take all my sins away. I invite you to come into my heart to be my Lord and Savior. Amen.</u>

In memory of my two sons, Mike and Jerry:

I Got Shoes

I got shoes you got shoes all of God's childrens got shoes
When I get to heaven gonna put on my shoes
I'm gonna walk all over God's heaven heaven
Everybody talkin' bout heaven ain't a goin' there heaven
heaven

I have a cross, you have a cross. All of God's childrens got a
cross.
When we get to heaven, we gonna lay down our cross
And run all over God's heaven, heaven
Everybody talking about heaven, heaven ain't going there
heaven.

I got a robe, you got a robe, all of God's childrens got a robe
When we get to heaven, we gonna take off our robes
And we gonna shout all over God's heaven.
Everybody talkin' bout heaven ain't a goin' there heaven
heaven

I'm gonna walk all over God's heaven (I'm gonna fly)
I got wings you got wings all of God's childrens got wings
When I get to heaven gonna put on my wings
I'm gonna fly all over God's heaven heaven
Everybody talkin' bout heaven ain't a goin' there heaven
heaven

I'm gonna fly all over God's heaven (it's gonna shine)
I got a crown you got a crown all of God's childrens got a
crown

When I get to heaven gonna put on my crown
I'm gonna shine all over God's heaven heaven
Everybody talkin' bout heaven ain't a goin' there heaven
heaven

I'm gonna shine all over God's heaven (I'm gonna play)
I got a harp you got a harp all of God's childrens got a harp
When I get to heaven gonna play on my harp
I'm gonna play all over God's heaven heaven
Everybody talkin' bout heaven ain't a goin' there heaven
heaven
I'm gonna play all over God's heaven
(I'm gonna walk fly shine play) walk all over God's heaven

About the author

Dorothy Coleman has had repeated visitations and visions since she became a born-again Christian and received the Holy Spirit with speaking in tongues. Her faith and her love of God is shown by miracles and the healing of others. She and her husband, Al, are chaplains and ministers who both regularly visit hospitals, nursing homes and private homes. They have an ongoing Bible Study in their home.

Dorothy has also been on radio sharing about the cross when she lived in California. She has played in powerful Drama The Great White Throne Judgment, and many people were saved. When she and Al moved to Texas they were on the news sharing about how Jesus healed Al of cancer.

In Texas, Dorothy had another opportunity to play in the Christmas Post. Three nights again many people came to Jesus. She currently resides in Arizona.

88857418R00057

Made in the USA
Columbia, SC
11 February 2018